Two Rivers

MĀNOA 14:1   **UNIVERSITY**   **HONOLULU**
                     OF HAWAI'I
                     PRESS

14. Tonkin
BAIE D'ALONG — Passe vers Port Wallut

Collection de l'Union Commercial Indochinoise

Two Rivers

NEW VIETNAMESE WRITING

FROM

AMERICA

AND

VIET NAM

Frank Stewart

EDITOR

Kevin Bowen
Nguyen Ba Chung

FEATURE EDITORS

Editor Frank Stewart

Managing Editor Pat Matsueda

Production Editors Liana Holmberg, Charlene Gilmore

Designer and Art Editor Barbara Pope

Fiction Editor Ian MacMillan

Poetry and Nonfiction Editor Frank Stewart

Associate Fiction Editor Susan Bates

Abernethy Apprentice Tamara Pavich

Staff Jenny Foster, Brent Fujinaka, Ryan Kawamoto, Naomi Long, Kathleen Matsueda, Alexander Mawyer, Celeste McCarthy, Amber Stierli

Corresponding Editors for North America
Fred Chappell, T. R. Hummer, Charles Johnson, Maxine Hong Kingston, Michael Ondaatje, Alberto Ríos, Arthur Sze, Tobias Wolff

Corresponding Editors for Asia and the Pacific
CHINA Howard Goldblatt, Ding Zuxin
HONG KONG Shirley Geok-lin Lim
INDONESIA John H. McGlynn
JAPAN Masao Miyoshi, Leza Lowitz
KOREA Kim Uchang, Bruce Fulton
NEW ZEALAND AND SOUTH PACIFIC Vilsoni Hereniko
PACIFIC LATIN AMERICA H. E. Francis, James Hoggard
PHILIPPINES Alfred A. Yuson
WESTERN CANADA Charlene Gilmore

Advisory Group Esther K. Arinaga, William H. Hamilton, Franklin S. Odo, Joseph O'Mealy, Robert Shapard, Marjorie Sinclair

Founded in 1988 by Robert Shapard and Frank Stewart.

Mānoa is published twice a year. Subscriptions: U.S.A. and Canada—individuals $22 one year, $40 two years. Other countries—individuals $25 one year, $45 two years. All countries—single copy $20; institutions $40 one year, $72 two years.

For air mail add $18 per year. Call toll free 1-888-UHPRESS. We accept checks, money orders, VISA, or MasterCard, payable to University of Hawai'i Press, 2840 Kolowalu Street, Honolulu, HI 96822, U.S.A. Claims for issues not received will be honored until 180 days past the date of publication; thereafter, the single-copy rate will be charged.

Mānoa is also available online through Project MUSE <http://muse.jhu.edu>.

Manuscripts may be sent to *Mānoa*, English Department, University of Hawai'i, Honolulu, HI 96822. Please include self-addressed, stamped envelope for return of manuscript or for our reply.

www.hawaii.edu/mjournal
www.uhpress.hawaii.edu/journals/manoa/

CONTENTS

Special Focus New Vietnamese Writing

Cliché de Sesmaisons

676. Un passage difficile dans le Nam-Kan (Haut-Tonkin) provinces frontières)

Editor's Note

Twice a year, *Mānoa*'s editors gather new writing from throughout Asia, Oceania, and the Americas. Each volume highlights authors of a particular country or region, placing them alongside other international writers of distinction. *Two Rivers,* guest-edited by Kevin Bowen and Nguyen Ba Chung, features works by contemporary Vietnamese and Vietnamese American writers.

Historically, Viet Nam has been a country of confluences—not only because of its two great waterways, the Red River in the north and the Mekong River in the south, but also because of the coming together of important cultures, religions, and ideas. Sometimes the confluences have been peaceful and at other times traumatic. The country has a lengthy history of being invaded and colonized, as well as being divided by political and military rivalries. Therefore, many streams and rivers crisscross and create change in this place where the words for *nation* and *water* are homonyms. In spite of differences in ideals and ideologies, the people of Viet Nam have maintained a sense of nationhood that has long withstood the powerful forces that would divide them.

Viet Nam's foundation myths bring together the concepts of unity and division. The narrative of the fifteenth-century collection *Linh-nam trich quai* describes the Vietnamese people as the offspring of a Dragon King, associated with Water, and an immortal woman, associated with the Mountains. The parents produced one hundred children, who were sent in opposite directions: half with their mother toward the northern mountains, and the other half with their father toward the southern sea. Though separated, the children were told to protect each other and to reunite in time of need. Separation, wandering, and homecoming have remained themes in the poetry and fiction of Viet Nam.

For over two thousand years, the children of the mountains and the waters reigned over the country they called Van Lang. For the next thousand years, the Chinese dominated and occupied the country, until they were driven out in the tenth century. There followed cycles of invasion—again by the Chinese and later by the French, the Japanese, and the Americans—and, after each wave of invaders, the reassertion of independence. In his story "Rivers," printed in this volume, Nguyen Qui Duc renders these cycles as a series of dreams flowing into one another, across time and geography: the Vietnamese-French War flows into the Vietnamese-American War, and both flow backwards into the triumphant expulsion of 200,000 Chinese troops by a smaller Vietnamese army in 1788.

Near the end of the twentieth century, Viet Nam endured one of its most traumatic periods of war and social displacement. When American forces withdrew from the Viet Nam conflict in 1973—an event that led to the collapse of the South Vietnamese government two years later—tens of thousands of refugees fled the country in anticipation of reprisals by the government of the North. Of this first wave of emigrants, about 130,000 settled in the United States. They included ex-soldiers, government officials, their families, and others who had supported the Southern cause. When they arrived on American shores, fewer than 20,000 Vietnamese were living here; thus, there were no Vietnamese support groups or large immigrant communities to help them adjust to their country of refuge and cope with defeat and displacement. Many had been educated professionals at home, but during their first years in America were forced to survive on menial jobs as they struggled to keep their families together and raise their children.

In the following decades, additional thousands of Vietnamese had reason to leave the homeland; waves of new emigrants made their way to America. In the late 1970s and early 1980s, an unknown number of so-called boat people fled Viet Nam's harsh, post-war economic conditions and a government policy of discrimination against ethnic Chinese citizens. Tens of thousands risked their lives at sea in unsafe vessels, and as many as half may have died; the more fortunate ones reached refugee camps throughout Southeast Asia. In some cases, people in these camps were detained, robbed, and brutalized for years before being sent back to Viet Nam or allowed to leave for third countries, which included the United States. By 1980, the number of Vietnamese in America had increased to 250,000.

Another group emigrating in the 1980s comprised thousands of men and women who had been labeled collaborators and traitors after the collapse of the South Vietnamese government. Many were imprisoned or forced to live in so-called New Economic Zones in the remote mountains and jungles, where they were harshly reeducated in the ideals of communism. In 1988, when the Vietnamese and u.s. governments came to an agreement that allowed for the release and departure of former political prisoners and detainees, an estimated 100,000 went abroad, many of them reuniting with relatives in America.

Other Vietnamese emigrants during this period consisted of children whose mothers were Vietnamese and fathers were American soldiers. Often impoverished, abandoned, and living on the streets in Viet Nam, the children were called *bui doi* (the dust of life), an expression referring to the abject poor. Despite the prejudice they suffered in their own country, and the responsibility that America shared for their predicament, it took considerable negotiation between the Vietnamese and U.S. governments before these children and their mothers were allowed to leave the country for the United States. As a result of the 1987 Amerasian Homecoming Act, almost 100,000 reached America and received refugee resettlement benefits; unfortunately, many still remain in Viet Nam.

Today, there are just over one million Vietnamese and Vietnamese Americans in the United States. In his overview essay for *Two Rivers,* "The Long Road Home: Exile, Self-Recognition, and Reconstruction," Nguyen Ba Chung describes their situation: the complex relationships among the various generations living here, and the changing attitudes of the Vietnamese living abroad toward the nearly eighty million residing in the homeland. During the past twenty-five years, some rifts have remained and even widened, while others have begun to close. For many in the older generation, the Vietnamese-American War can never be forgotten and the victors never forgiven; for others, the war has become a terrible, sad fact that must be relegated to past. For those too young to remember it, the war is ancient history. This last group is slowly becoming the majority as their elders, both here and in Viet Nam, pass away.

Two Rivers features works of poetry and prose that represent each of these points of view and the many perspectives in between.

Andrew Lam's story in this volume, "Fire," portrays a man of the generation that fought for South Viet Nam during the Vietnamese-American War. Now living in America, the man is torn between his generation's loyalty to the country it lost and his loyalty to his family, which has been altered by its adopted home. With the death of his oldest and closest friend —someone who was determined to keep old loyalties alive—he may finally be able to accept and even embrace the present.

"Better Homes and Gardens," by Viet Thanh Nguyen, tells the story of a Vietnamese youth with adoptive Wisconsin parents. He had hoped he would be a "wide-eyed and thankful orphan boy." Instead, he can't overcome a past that includes "men slaughtered, women gang-raped, and hope lost on a refugee boat that had wandered in the South China Sea."

In Nguyen Minh Chau's "The Self-Portrait," personal and political destinies become entangled, and self-knowledge about one's own hypocrisy in time of war ultimately overwhelms a man and becomes his burden.

Mike Ngo's story "A Day in the Life" depicts a burden of war that travels from father to son. Here, the Vietnamese American narrator daily confronts the irony of his father's escaping imprisonment in the homeland only to have his son imprisoned in the country to which he fled for refuge. Wondering how his fellow inmates view him, the incarcerated narrator says, "They probably see what I see every morning in my pocket-sized mirror toothpasted to the wall: my father, a veteran who lost his country, and his dreams."

Hoang Lien's poem "Crossing the Parallel" begins, "March, march on, on this endless path." Hoang describes a path carved by the passage of men and an "ill-willed river / That divides a nation in half, its water running in two different courses." The conflict between choice and destiny cuts especially deep for men such as Hoang, who fought for South Viet Nam and was imprisoned by the North. In his poem "In the Same Boat," he speaks powerfully of "the homeland . . . so far yet so near, / so deep in our heart."

Other Vietnamese and Vietnamese American poets in *Two Rivers* are Du Tu Le, Truong Tran, Barbara Tran, Mộng-Lan, Lam Thi My Da, Huu Thinh, Mai Thao, Do Kh., Le Bi, Phan Nhien Hao, and Tran Tien Dung. One of the best known, Mai Thao writes movingly of "departed spirits [that] wake up inside me, / . . . set off wildfires and floods in my heart."

Viet Nam's most popular songwriter during the war years was Trinh Cong Son. With compassion and courage, he wrote about the country's social and political troubles while also composing ballads of love and personal longing. Trinh took the side of neither the government of the North nor of the South; he was banned by each and imprisoned. He sided instead with the Vietnamese people and with all those who suffered as a result of war. For *Two Rivers*, Frank Gerke contributes an essay on Trinh Cong Son, and Nguyen Qui Duc translates five of his songs.

Two Rivers also includes Chinese poet Guo Lusheng, who is the subject of an essay by Zhang Lijia, "Mad Dog: The Legend of Chinese Poet Guo Lusheng." Living in relative isolation in a house for the mentally ill—his psychosis due in some degree to political persecution during the Cultural Revolution—Guo says: "I'm not allowed to read books. And this terrible environment leaves me longing for beautiful things. I believe that when your bitterness reaches its peak, your soul becomes perfect."

Other writers in this volume speak in equally poignant and unsentimental ways about the confluences of history and of the heart, and of the fundamental desire to hold on to what poet Leonard Nathan calls the "voices of smoke."

Fire

Mister Cao's oolong tea from Guangdong was wasted that woeful Thanksgiving morning; special tea though it was, it was sipped wearily. As usual, we sat at our corner table at the Golden Phoenix, Mister Cao's restaurant, chatting quietly, when Mister Huy ran in as if chased by a ghost. "Undone, absolutely undone!" he yelled, waving the *San Jose Mercury News* expressively above his bald head. "Mister Bac has committed self-immolation."

"Self-immolation?" I mumbled, and the words vibrated in my throat and swirled between my ears, reigniting that terrifying flame of long ago. The flame blossomed quickly, a flower on fire, a restless, transparent bird of paradise in whose pistil a Buddhist monk sat serenely. "Self-immolation!" I repeated. The meaning sank in finally, the flame soared and wavered, and the monk fell backward. His charred body went into a spasm or two and then was perfectly still. "Oh God!" I said. "No!"

Mister Cao in the meanwhile had stood up and snatched the newspaper from Mister Huy's hand as if the two of them were engaged in some desultory septuagenarian game of relay. "Are you joking?!" he yelled. Heads turned. His three waiters in their red jackets and black bow ties paused in their tracks, their trays balancing precariously on industrious fingers. The restaurant, too, fell into a hushed murmur, all eyes trained on us. "How can this be?" he asked. "I just had lunch with him here last Monday!"

Mister Huy shook his head and sighed. "Read, read," he said. He was almost out of breath; tiny beads of perspiration glistened on his age-spotted forehead. "Mister Bac went all the way to Washington, D.C., to do it."

What immediately struck me were not the words themselves but the two photographs that accompanied the article. The larger was a blurry image of a figure on fire, a human torch swirling in a fiery circle on a landing of the Capitol building, his face lifted skyward, arms raised above his head as if waiting for a benediction from the heavens. The smaller was the photo of Nguyen Hoai Bac's driver's license, the image I readily recognized: Old Silver Eagle, publisher of the *Viet Nam Forever,* smiling with mischievous eyes at the camera. As I studied the two disparate photos—life versus death—I heard Mister Cao say rather impatiently, "Out loud, Thang, read it out loud! Please, you're the professor."

Thus, on that decrepit morning, with the oolong's bittersweet aftertaste on my palate and a crowd gathering around me, I heard myself recite in English what turned out to be my oldest and dearest friend's obituary.

Late Wednesday afternoon a man doused himself in gasoline, marched up the steps of the Capitol building and, upon reaching the first landing, lit a match. John Lerner, a tourist from North Dakota, managed to capture a photo (see far right) of the self-immolator, who was later identified by the police as Bac Hoai Nguyen, 65, a Vietnamese American and an editor and publisher of a Viet-namese-language magazine in San Jose, California.

According to his youngest daughter, Theresa Nguyen, 21, a senior at Georgetown University, Mister Nguyen did not give any indication as to what he was about to do. "He said he came to visit me since I couldn't go home for Thanksgiving," she reported through tears. "Then this morning he borrowed my Georgetown U sweatshirt and my car keys. He said he wanted to go for a walk around the monuments, but he never came home."

The article went on to say that Mister Bac had left a suicide note, which the paper translated and printed as a sidebar. So at the urging of my friends, I skipped the rest of the reporting and read our friend's last words and testimony:

Letter to the people of the free world,
Communism has ruined my country. My homeland is in shambles. I am tormented by thoughts of my people living in despair under the cruel commu-nist regime. I cannot sleep at night thinking about their suffering. I close my eyes and all I see are boat people drowning in the South China Sea and dissi-dents languishing in horrid prison conditions.

Human-rights violations in Viet Nam are among the worst in the world. I denounce its reeducation camps, its malaria-infested New Economic Zones and its continuing arrests of clergymen and intellectuals without due process.

I have lived a full life. I have been blessed with comforts and a supportive family. But considering the plight of my people, I cannot be so selfish as to live the remains of my days in peace. My conscience demands that I act and offer myself completely to the cause of my country.

May my insignificant body serve as a little flame that shines in the darkness that has befallen my country. May my death reveal to the civilized world the evil of the communist ideology and godless demons who continue to drink the blood of my people.

I wish you all a healthy, peaceful and prosperous life.
Good-bye,
Nguyen Hoai Bac

Mister Bac's words hung in the air long after I finished reading them. Feeling strangely parched and utterly exhausted, I took a deep breath. Exhaled. Took another. Exhaled even slower. But this calming exercise learned from my long-dead father to combat my childhood bouts with asthma had the opposite effect that day. For instead of feeling calm I—

after more than a dozen or so years after quitting—imagined a cigarette smoldering between my lips. I could almost feel its smoky residues warming my variegated lungs.

For sometime now, a salty beam of sunlight had come slanting through the opaque glass window and lit our Formica-topped table, highlighting our sorrowful and ruined faces. Mister Cao was struggling to keep from sobbing, his long and deeply wrinkled face a map of pain; Mister Huy, in the manner of a hurt child, was intermittently wiping his teary eyes with the backs of his hands.

A profound sadness welled up from deep inside me, too, and I had to close my eyes. I heard a child's cry, a woman's shrill laughter, men's low bantering and speculating voices. I smelled that complex aroma of *pho* soup—its beef broth spiced with star anise—and freshly roasted coffee scenting the air. Everything was the same that morning, yet everything had changed. When I opened my eyes again and looked at Mister Bac's chair, I saw an unspeakable void. It forced me to look away, out the window, to the busy sun-drenched thoroughfare of Santa Clara. What I saw was smeared with my own tears. Old Silver Eagle, poor soul, was really gone!

When I think of him, "the first" is always what comes to mind. The first to start a newspaper in exile—right in the Guam refugee camp, as a matter of fact—with sets of Vietnamese type he had brought with him on his escape from Saigon. The first to organize an anticommunist rally in San Jose; the first to put together cultural shows and Tet festivals on the Santa Clara fairgrounds; and, as it turned out, the first—and only—to commit self-immolation in America to protest Vietnamese communism.

A restless spirit, Mister Bac always pleaded and urged many to "do something for our homeland," if not "for future generations." Have we, he often asked, forgotten the past? Who among us hadn't suffered under communist hands? Are we so afraid, so near to the grave, we can't speak up?

Imagine, then, four old men in black pajamas sitting inside a flimsy bamboo cage at Vietnamese-owned Lion Plaza, located at the end of Tully Road, protesting Ha Noi's unjustifiable arrests of clergymen and dissidents back home. The cage was so flimsy that my adorable seven-year-old granddaughter, Kimmy, could break out with ease, and her equally adorable four-year-old brother, Aaron, could squeeze through without touching the bars. Still, for four straight days and three consecutive nights, we starved. The South Vietnamese flag—three blood-red horizontal stripes on a gold background—flapped heroically in the summer wind. Shoppers walked by and waved hello, and children giggled as they stared at the sight. We would talk to anyone regarding the decrepit state of Viet Nam, the cruelty of life under communist oppression, and so on. Young supporters stood by and passed out literature on the subject, and a few shoppers even posed with us for photographs.

Still, as far as hunger strikes go, it no doubt ranked among the Rolls

Royces. After all, how many political prisoners back home had Old Cao's cellular phone, which he'd brought so that he could instruct his restaurant staff? And it is very doubtful that those prisoners were provided with sleeping bags and pillows by caring relatives. Trang, my sweet and loving wife, scented mine with her trademark Toujours Moi perfume to remind me that this old goat had something to come home to. Last but not least, how many had a cardiologist—to be exact, my youngest son, whom my wife and I now live with—who'd come out and monitor their heart rate and blood pressure daily? True, Tinh wouldn't fail to chastise our act of protest as "pure folly" and "most unhealthy," and each of us had to promise him that it would end soon. When we made the front page of the *San Jose Mercury News* on the fourth morning, the hunger protest mercifully ended.

Or so we thought.

How would we know that Old Silver Eagle would take it to its fiery and bitter end?

That afternoon we saw a procession of mourners at the Golden Phoenix. Old friends and acquaintances, strangers who heard the news dropped in by the dozens to express their shock and dismay. But this procession ended when Miss Sally Bernstein from the *Mercury News* came striding in. There was something in her appearance, I suppose—the bright blond hair that gleamed in the sunlight, painted red lips, piercing blue eyes, a confident stride—that turned heads. She moved, that is to say, the way a hungry shark would among a school of frightened tunas.

Miss Sally smiled and greeted each one of us by shaking hands. She was terribly sorry about "Mister Nguyen," but since his family was too upset to talk to the press, would we? She was doing a follow-up, "a local angle," as it were, on the story of his fiery demise and had been told that we were his closest friends, so would we care to shed some light on the matter?

Certainly, we answered. Of course, we said. Mister Cao played host. He promptly ordered another tea cup, some dry squid, and, as the mood caught him, a bottle of Courvoisier cognac and snifters for anyone who wanted to join him in commemorating Mister Bac. Then we proceeded to tell her about his background, his life, and, above all, how he lived a hero and died a martyr.

Miss Sally diligently took notes, saying "Uh-huh, uh-huh" and "yes, yes," but the heroic life of Mister Bac was not exactly what interested her, alas. Five minutes or so into it, she raised her pen and stopped us. "I have to say that Americans don't understand this form of protest at all," she said. What she was after was his motive or, perhaps, motives. "For instance, the publisher of the *Saigon Today* suggested that Mister Bac Nguyen was facing bankruptcy due to his lack of readers and advertisements. That he committed suicide out of desperation and deep depression. I checked it out this morning, and he did file for bankruptcy last week. Can anyone here, *uhm*, speak about this?"

The news stunned us. What the American reporter heard next was a collective groan. I, for one, never liked that *Saigon Today* publisher: a young upstart computer engineer with lots of money to throw around. His rag of a magazine, by the way, is full of gossip and lewd-looking Vietnamese starlets. But his attack on Mister Bac's good name less than a day after his fiery demise was insulting to the bone.

Miss Sally's question galvanized our thoughts and feelings. "Motives? But there's only one," intoned Mister Huy with all seriousness. Once a judge in the municipal court in Saigon, he could be imposing when necessary, and he certainly rose to the occasion. "He lived for Viet Nam and he died for Viet Nam. What else is there to know? Why go digging for things that do not exist?"

"Agreed, agreed," added Mister Cao, "a hero and a role model."

Drawing inspiration from the old days when I lectured in Saigon on Vietnamese history—one full of heroes and strife—I told her that I knew nothing about the bankruptcy, that Mister Bac never mentioned it. Not to me, not to Mister Cao, or to Mister Huy. We saw him last, I said, only a week earlier, and we shook hands and promised to meet as usual here at the Phoenix, and he was as calm as a frozen lake in winter.

I told her that I knew no one more dedicated to the cause of human rights in Viet Nam than our recently departed comrade. He lived fighting for freedom and justice in Viet Nam, so why shouldn't he die calling for attention to those causes? After all, who among us didn't suffer under communism? Mister Huy lost his wife when they fled by boat in '79 to Thailand. Mister Cao lost his brother to a Viet Cong's bullet in '67. And Mister Bac's parents were executed as landowners in Son Tay. And last but not least, there was me. I lost my first son, Tuyen, who never made it past his twenty-first birthday, in '74, a year before the war ended—and ended badly for us all. And as far as I was concerned, Mister Bac spoke his heart and mind in the letter that the *Mercury* published. The Vietnamese exile community, I said, owes him an enormous debt for his selflessness and should commemorate his passing.

"Well spoken," Mister Huy said.

"Bravo," Mister Cao said and applauded.

Miss Sally knit her brows, bit her lower lip, and gave the impression of making a half pout. "I'm sorry," she announced obliquely, "I do have materials about his accomplishments. But if you don't mind, I'd still like to have some sense of his state of mind. I mean, do you think the way he committed suicide characteristic of who he was?"

"Not suicide, not suicide," Mister Huy corrected her. He tapped his tea cup on the table top repeatedly, perhaps imagining it a gavel. "You mean sacrifice. *Sa-cri-fice*. Mister Bac was a martyr. He sacrificed his life for Viet Nam."

Miss Sally nodded, but she seemed to be smirking slightly, perhaps finding the point trivial. She was about to ask another question when Mister Cao, irked by her expression, stood up and raised his snifter with his eyes glazed over and his voice full of lamentation. "Brother Bac," he said in Vietnamese, "let me drink to your bravery regardless of what others say or think. You are a shining example to our community and our country."

Mister Cao joined him. The two began to address Mister Bac's ghost directly and ignored Miss Sally altogether. Their voices grew sadder and more plaintive with each toast.

"Brother Bac, may your ghost return to Viet Nam and haunt all those bastards in Ha Noi in their sleep."

"Come back, brother, and witness this tragedy. You're not even buried and people are already slandering your name. So much for gratitude. Damn it all."

So on and so on.

Miss Sally, I must say, looked both confused and embarrassed. She intermittently scratched the nape of her neck and smoothed her hair as she watched. Even if she expected resistance with her line of questioning, I doubt that she was prepared for what must have appeared to her a Vietnamese mass seance.

Then it was my turn. Perhaps I wanted to outdo them, carried away as I was by my previous soliloquy. Perhaps that was why I said it. I stood and ceremoniously raised my snifter to Mister Bac, and in a low, solemn, pained voice, I said, "Brother, don't be surprised if I follow in your brave footsteps. We'll show the Americans—and not to mention the younger generation—what old men are capable of." But before I drank the cognac, Mister Cao and Mister Huy made such a commotion that I knew I had misspoken. Miss Sally, true to her profession, immediately asked both of them what I had just said, and Mister Huy promptly translated. She looked at me then with great interest. "Is it true, sir, that you're also considering self-immolation?"

"Well, no, I mean, I might," I stammered, but the conviction with which I had addressed Old Silver Eagle's spirit had escaped me. Inwardly, I began to fret that I would be quoted in the paper and that there would be consequences. I could see my wife's disapproving face, and I couldn't bear it. Still, it was too late; the words were launched. "If I think it necessary—that is, if it brings changes to Viet Nam—I would do it," I added.

"Oh, I see," said Miss Sally, disappointed. "Forgive me, but if you, his closest friend, couldn't be sure that your death would bring changes to Viet Nam, then how can you argue so adamantly on behalf of Mister Bac Nguyen?"

I didn't answer, for at that moment Mister Cao decided to save me from Miss Sally. He rose and with verve started to sing the South Vietnamese national anthem. I could almost see him as a captain in his paratrooper's uniform and red beret—a young panther way back when. His face was red, his voice deep and strong, and it managed to startle everyone once more.

> *Oh citizens! Let's rise up*
> *the day of liberation is here!*
> *With a single resolve*
> *let us go sacrifice our*
> *lives under the flag.*

Personally, I'd rather have gone on answering Miss Sally's questions, defending myself and, if possible, challenging some of her dark notions. But thanks to Mister Cao, I wasn't given much of a choice. Out of respect for the anthem, I also stood up and joined my friends in song. Half of the customers at the Phoenix and even the three well-trained waiters with black bow ties joined in.

Miss Sally shrank a little in her chair. Journalists have to dig deep, I know, but digging deep with us old men often results in bent spades and broken shovels.

The drama, however, did not end in a stalemate, as I'd hoped. If there was anyone to spoil it all for us, it was, I regret to report, my son Tinh, known to our community as Doctor Tony Tran, the cardiologist. Tinh's arrival changed everything.

Tinh and I should have gone home, but old Huy, drunk now and bold, decided to introduce him: "Doctor Tony Tran—so successful but too bad married, *haha!*" Miss Sally immediately latched on to my son, married or not, like a leech to a farmer's leg. She had questions regarding Mister Bac's death, his state of mind, and so on, and was wondering if my son wouldn't mind answering them.

Tinh glanced at me, then flashed his apologetic smile and said, "Actually, we're kind of in a hurry. My wife and mother have been cooking all day. And the kids are wondering when Grandpapa is coming home. It's Thanksgiving, you know."

To encourage his good sense, I began to gather my hat and scarf, but Miss Sally did not give up. "Just one question, please, it's important," she said, and before Tinh agreed to it, she asked anyway. "Even among the Vietnamese I interviewed, opinions varied. Some people said that it was an act of madness, others that it was heroic. Your father said it's an act of ultimate bravery. In fact, he said that he would consider committing this act himself if he deemed it necessary."

The vixen! Oh, how my heart jumped! I nearly dropped my hat. Distracted, I fumbled through my sports jacket's empty pockets as if looking for a pack of cigarettes, or perhaps a gun—to commit either suicide or murder.

"He said *what?*" Tinh asked. A dark color came over his handsome face and instead of helping me up, he grabbed another chair and sat himself down. "Well, Sally, you know what," he said, pretending to look at his watch, "I do have a few minutes to spare."

"Oh, thank you," said Miss Sally, beaming, "and would you say something about his state of mind as well."

I cleared my throat. "I thought we were late," I said, but no one heard me.

"Let me preface it by saying that I do not support any sort of protest that can do oneself physical harm, including, of course, hunger strikes," my son said. "I've been thinking about Mister Nguyen's death since I heard the news. Personally, I have always respected him for his work. But to live fighting for something is different from dying in its name, especially when it is absolutely uncalled for.

"As to his state of mind, I wonder . . . A newspaperman like him—why would he do it on the afternoon before Thanksgiving? It's one of the lone-liest days in D.C. Were he of sound mind, Mister Nguyen would have remembered that the media and Congress and their staff are already gone, that Capitol Hill is but an empty structure. I hate to be so cynical about it —but you can't protest like this twice. So, not that he should have, but why not do it on a Monday morning and waylay that fat candidate for a triple bypass Speaker of the House what's-his-name on his way to lunch? Surely *that* would get the attention of all the major newspapers across the country, not to mention television coverage—say, CNN and commentaries in the opinion-editorial pages of the *Washington Post* and *New York Times*. If he really intended to call the world's attention to the cause of Viet Nam, why would he shy away from the world at the very end?"

My son went on, but I'd stopped listening. He was venting his anger at me—that was obvious—but did Mister Bac's name have to be dragged in the mud in the process? What to do? Nothing. Absolutely nothing. To fight with him in front of Miss Sally and the Golden Phoenix crowd was to convey to the public the discordance within my family. So I sat and marveled instead at my growing resentment of America: how she snatches immigrant and refugee children from their parents' bosoms and turns them into sophisticated, razor-tongued strangers.

On our way home we were very, very quiet.

Tinh drove calmly, his right index finger dancing back and forth in vivacious arcs above the leather-bound steering wheel while Vivaldi's *Four Seasons* followed one another in inevitable succession. I noted his hands then—strong but ordinary—and wondered, How many sternum had they cracked? How many tender hearts had they massaged and mended? How many had they failed altogether?

The more beautiful the music, the more I found being in his car unbear-able. "Well," I said finally, "I hope you're happy. Tomorrow our community will think our family a miserable lot." Tinh turned to me and feigned surprise. "Sorry, Father. I don't understand."

"You understand perfectly: if you don't watch your mouth, you won't have any Vietnamese clients left. Our people will boycott your office for what you said today. They'll wave flags in front of your clinic and call you a communist sympathizer—that's what I'm saying."

My son sighed deeply, but when he spoke, his voice had a tinge of sarcasm. "Do you mean to suggest that my Vietnamese patients would rather stay home and suffer coronary blockages, arrhythmias, and strokes simply because I disagreed with you? Let me ask you this, Father: how many doctors in their right mind would prescribe self-immolation as a healthy form of venting one's anger at cruel history?"

"Oh, don't pretend to be so naive," I said, matching venom with venom. "You're not the only cardiologist in town, even with your good reputation —a reputation which, I might add, is about to be smeared. You know the community. Gossip abounds, fingers are easily pointed on the basis of mere rumor. Tomorrow we'll be a laughingstock. I can see Miss Sally's writing up that wretched article right now as we speak: SON DISAGREES WITH FATHER OVER FIERY PROTEST—GENERATIONAL RIFT IN VIETNAMESE COMMUNITY.

Tinh shook his head lightly. He has that way of disapproving of someone without saying a word—a trait inherited, surely, from his recalcitrant mother. "Father, I simply questioned whether it was worth dying for something you believe in instead of living and fighting for it. It's a question of logic. All right, I concede that I may have sounded disrespectful but—"

Before he could finish his sentence, I slapped the polished wooden dashboard in front of me, and the noise it made, like a small explosion, startled us both. I couldn't help it; my anger had boiled over. "Please! No more. No more of this logic. I don't want to hear any damn logic. My best friend just died, and my son called him a lunatic in public. How am I to take it? How am I going to show my face at the Golden Phoenix now that my son has derided the dead?"

Tinh said nothing but sent yet another sigh my way, and silence was temporarily restored. As soon as we came to a quiet neighborhood, however, he parked the Jaguar to the side rather abruptly and then reached for the *Mercury News* in the back seat. "Listen, Father," he said as he unfolded the paper, his voice rising, "let's get it off our chests, shall we, before we go home for a lovely family dinner?"

I said nothing, a little surprised that he stopped the car in the middle of nowhere. "Good," he said, monitoring my expression. "For one thing, don't damn logic, I beg you. Passion without logic can lead you astray. I did not call Uncle Bac a lunatic and you know it, but I'm afraid the rest of the world might think so. Listen to this: this is the guy who took that photo—Mr. Lerner somebody. This is what he said: 'At first I thought it

Lam . Fire   9

was a flag-burning protest. Only when I zoomed my camera did I realize that it was some guy on fire. It's madness!'"

Tinh looked at me rather triumphantly. At that moment, I felt like an unfortunate, helpless old man, someone caught in a Confucian tragedy wherein son lectures father. "It *is* absolute madness, Father," he said, his voice admonishing me. "If that tourist wasn't there, Uncle Bac's story would have been on page 5 with two paragraphs at the most, if that. Father, you know what I think? I think that ultimately he was selfish, suffering from an incurable martyr complex, and it robbed him of his common sense. Did he do his daughter, Theresa, any favor? Or his suffering wife? His friends? And is that what you want, Father, to be 'some guy on fire'? Do you seriously want to be remembered by Kimmy and Aaron that way? Do you want to die so that you don't have to go on hurting from what was robbed from you—from us?"

We looked at each other then, stunned. He had spoken one sentence too many, and he knew it. How ironic: my son argued for logic, but what erupted from underneath that cool, polished demeanor was the deep sorrow we shared. His eyes swelled with tears, and his voice was all choked up as the last sentence spilled out of him.

A dam broke. I again saw Tuyen's coffin being lowered into the ground, saw his handsome, smiling face peering out of a black-and-white photo behind white snapdragons and daffodils on the wooden altar, as if trying to speak to the living. I saw, too, burnt paper offerings at his newly covered grave and incense smoke billowing against a gray sky, and my wife crouching in her white mourning *ao dai* dress as she wept and my youngest son hugged himself from all the pain, the grief. I began to itch all over. I couldn't stand to be inside that luxury car any longer. I felt parched and heated. Before I knew it, I had opened the door and climbed out.

"What are you doing?!" Tinh asked. "It's freezing out. Father! . . . Father?"

I said nothing. I started walking.

A few steps, and I felt a gentle grip on my elbow and turned to see my son looking at me, bewildered, his breath a wafting cloud between us. "Please, Ba," he said in a very different tone of voice now, the kind that he used to speak to me when he was young; that is to say, intimate and without rancor. "Ba, please, come back inside. I'm sorry. Really, I went too far just now, I know. It's just that . . . Oh, never mind. Ba, please, Ba! Huyen and Mother have been cooking all day, and the children are waiting."

But I said in my stern, determined voice, "Look, you go home first. I just need a good walk."

My son studied my face for a second or two and relented. He took off his overcoat and draped it over my shoulders. And I did not refuse his kindness. I put my arms through its sleeves and began walking. For several blocks he trailed me in his car, driving as slow as a turtle and being honked at repeatedly by drivers who then zoomed angrily past him. To put an end to his pious pursuit, I turned down a one-way street, away from the direction of our house.

I kept moving. The streets opened themselves to me as if they were an entirely new landscape. What was vaguely familiar from the view of a moving car or bus turned foreign while one was on foot. Branches hung over the sidewalk, their leaves rustling in the wind. When an odor of burning wood from someone's fireplace reached my nostrils, I was momentarily seized by an inexplicable sense of longing and nostalgia.

At a neighborhood grocery store, I purchased my first pack of cigarettes in many, many years, as well as a lighter. I leaned against a tree and smoked. The taste? Disgusting. Or should I say, Wonderfully disgusting? Like an old lover's kiss. The smoke burned the membrane in the back of my throat, seared my lungs, and made my body convulse. I coughed, spat, felt deliciously guilty for breaking my vow to my wife, but this was an emergency. When I was done with my first, I lit yet another. By the third, it felt as if I had never given up. How I missed the way the plumes escaped from my mouth and nostrils and into the ether.

I resumed walking. Twilight, and the world—leaves, walls, roofs, grass, windows, barren trees, and parked cars—bathed once more in that violent radiance of dusk.

I didn't know where I was going. But I kept moving as night fell. In my unsettled mind, I saw Mister Bac as in a newsreel: swirling in slow motion, cocooned in a flickering fire. I kept thinking, Did he scream? How painful was it? Did he cry for help? Or did he die like Thich Quang Duc, that holy monk of 1963, muted and ethereal as a statue of an orator?

My son's question plagued me. *Where should love for country end, and where should common sense begin?*

Could I pour gasoline on myself and light a match? Should I? Why should I? I could see myself running into a burning building to save my grandchildren without thinking twice, but I am not so unsophisticated as to dismiss my son's logic, or to be unaware that what I did in San Jose or Washington, D.C., carried very little weight, if any, in Ha Noi. Still, if I knew for sure my death would bring freedom to my people, I would do it gladly. But how could I ever be sure? I couldn't, despite what I told that wretched Miss Sally.

A car approached. Its bright headlights woke me from my torments. I squinted and thought for a second that it was my son coming back for me, but it passed by without slowing. When it was gone, I felt so disappointed that I nearly wept. I stared longingly toward where it had come from, but all I saw was an empty, dimly lit street that stretched toward an indecipherable darkness.

What surprised me most then, what I didn't dare think about until that moment was that, along with the sadness weighing down my heart, there was something else: a feeling that was hidden inside a turbulent sea and that only made itself whole when I was entirely alone and, apparently, very lost. I do not wish to say it, but I suppose I must. It was a sense of relief. There, I've said it. No more hunger strikes, no more talking to the press, no more shaking fists in the air and waving flags and banners, no more wearing black pajamas and posing for photographers. Without Old Silver Eagle, I would just sit at home from now on and tell my grandchildren fairy tales with sad endings and adventure stories of my youth.

I felt so ashamed and exasperated at this strange, selfish thought that I stopped walking. I couldn't move. I stood like that in the middle of nowhere for a long time until I heard what sounded like flapping wings. I turned. A piece of newspaper caught in a tiny whirlwind danced hauntingly before me. For almost half a minute, it glided up and down, down and up, graceful and elegant as a winged ballerina. A flock of dead maple leaves accompanied it in an eddy of air, and the sound of their rustling was melodic to my ears.

Finally, the twirling ended and the paper came to rest against a wire fence, where it flapped like some snared, wounded bird. I stared at it and found myself overcome with an inexplicable desire to set it free. But instead of picking it up, I childishly squatted down next to it, and then, like a crazed arsonist, I took out my lighter and lit its corner. On the second try, the fire caught and spread: a brilliant, mysterious flower undulating in the night.

I reached out then to the flame, not knowing what I was doing exactly—seeking, perhaps, to still my mind or find solace from the cold or communion with the dead. But to my surprise, my hand retracted instinctively at the first searing. The pain exploded inside my head, and I saw that holy monk once more falling backward, and I saw fiery napalm lighting the night sky. I saw burning buildings and heard the screams of children, and I felt as if my blood had somehow turned into lava and my heart was melted ore. I started weeping. I saw myself in all my contradictions: I hate those who caused my son's death, but I love my family more; I will never be free from the landscape of my earliest desires, yet as old as I was, I had no desire to give myself absolutely to that tumultuous past, even if it continued to rule me. I could never forget; yet how I yearned to be free from the hunger of memories.

I stared into the flickering fire, mesmerized. How many thousand years has man been staring into it, inspired, awed? How long have I? All my life, I suppose. This thing, this gift and curse, is a terrifying beauty, and though it had devoured my best friend, it would not, could not devour me. Contained, it hints of elegance, engines our world; out of control, it engulfs cities, souls, flesh. It creates. It seduces. It overpowers. It attracts. And it destroys.

The flame flickered and died before me. The crackling paper was now but an ultra thin, fragile skin the color of night. At my clumsy touch, it crumbled into bits and fragments and began to scatter in the wind. And for some reason, I found this to be utterly, inexplicably astonishing. And I found myself laughing. How tenuous everything was; yet, at the same time, how extraordinary.

I took a deep breath. I struggled to my feet, my joints aching. I looked about. My seared fingers throbbed painfully. It seemed that I had entered an elegant neighborhood where I had never been before. Satellite dishes sat on tiled rooftops; unknown trees and shrubs wavered under a starry sky. I felt like a thief in the night. I began to look into the lighted houses and saw that the holiday had begun. A well-dressed couple in one house was busy over the dining table, and at one point the man stood behind his wife and hugged her waist while hiding his face in the rich bloom of her reddish-brown hair, and this quickened my heart. In the next house, eight or nine people sat around a dining table, listening intently to a thin old woman with a shock of white hair. Wearing a blue blouse and standing behind a large roasted turkey at the far end of the table, she stretched out her arms and sang. When she was done, the people applauded, then raised their glasses merrily.

A whiff of roasted meat reached me then, and I found myself salivating. I inhaled deeply, and my stomach growled. I exhaled. I felt hunger pangs. So I moved on.

I kept moving.

Three Poems

QUIETUDE

As my crossed legs freeze to the thick stone floor
I no longer feel the spinning earth.
I have sat motionless for two years in one spot,
Night after night watching the moon wax and wane
And constellations faithfully bloom every evening
Beyond the trellis of thin bars on the jail window,
An indelible image of stillness
Undisturbed even by the drifting clouds.

In pain and sorrow I sit here,
Placid amidst the moon and stars.
No ocean's storm or hurricane
Can disturb the high hilltop I am on.

I sit in this temporal world
While moonlight purifies my soul.
The terrestrial pink dust that settles outside the prison door
Does not stain my gray prisoner's shirt.

I sit here while my cold and numb heart
Continually kindles its fire of faithfulness,
Even though my flesh and bone may turn to stone,
Like that rock that resembles the fabled mother holding her son
Watching for the return of her forever-absent husband
Frozen in her eternal wait atop the mountain.

Translation by Phon-anh

CROSSING THE PARALLEL

March, march on, on this endless path
That does not cease its climb up the Truong Son range.
Leaves are woven into branches, the trees tall and taller still;
Sunlight, in bright fragments like flowers, chases my footsteps;
The angry water of the falls flows violently down and downward—
But where to, and does it not carry shades of the homeland?
And will it flow into the ill-willed river
That divides a nation in half, its water running in two different
    courses?
My feet fall apart; the walking stick I can no longer hold.
My throat has burned dry, lips melted into one,
While my heart beats fast and my breathing bursts my lungs.
Still the mountain pass is high above,
And my steps cannot be slowed.

Move, move on—I am forced from my mother's land,
My exile's steps bloodied, my heart wounded,
While around me are tides of enmity;
White into black, even absolute truths have been perverted.

The afternoon folds its wings over this desolate jungle;
Let us pause, this moment, where birds and streams meet like lovers.
I do not fear these formidable miles
For I am this very night on the free shores still.

These flickering flames fail to make ashes of my sorrow;
The wind insists on blowing separation into my faithful soul.
My Southern land, will I ever return to you?
Or will my faith not blossom, red as the poincianas along the River
    of Perfume?

IN THE SAME BOAT

The sunset spreads, an exquisite gray robe,
The clouds cling, the wind blows, leaves wait for flowers;
Elsewhere, the weather may shine in glory,
Here in this drab spring afternoon, I am filled with longing.

Forty narrow rooms, so much suffering;
Separated by walls thick as miles
We each glimpse a piece of blue sky between green leaves
And wonder in what direction our home lies.

We dream of white rivers, golden sunlight,
Sweet coconut and palm trees spreading bountiful shade,
Of lotus flowers carrying the capital's past in their fragrance
Of a Lam Vien dusk lending a shade of purple to the peach blossoms.

Someone longs for his white-haired father,
Another a mother's tearful eyes,
A wife's face upon a solitary pillow,
And the dry lips of a child.

Our cause reverberates in me like ocean waves,
And I hear battle sounds from the Southern front;
Resenting my presence beyond the frontier
I hear too the echoes of distant guns.

In the same boat, we're lost without a landing dock,
Our longing stretching for a thousand miles to more longing.
The homeland is so far yet so near,
So deep in our heart.

Translations by Nguyen Qui Duc

Two Poems

WHEN I DIE TAKE MY BODY TO THE SEA

when I die, take my body to the sea
an exile's life must end without a grave
buried in a strange land a corpse may not dissolve
free the soul to find its way home

when I die, take my body to the sea
the ebbing tide will carry it away
across the ocean to the land of my birth
where bamboo hedges remain forever green

when I die, take my body to the sea
don't close the eyelids yet though, please
let me turn one last time towards home
who knows, my body might arrive there someday

when I die, take my body to the sea
don't for a single second pity me
so many drowned become food for fish
what can one more twisted corpse matter

when I die, take my body to the sea
send me home to catch sight of my children
send me home to see the tears in their eyes —
now sadder than even the darkness of night

when I die, take my body to the sea
on the way sing me the old nation's anthem
for so long no one has bothered to sing it
it's become a ghost tune

when I die, the sadness will die with me
an exile's life, true to the soul to the end

A POEM FOR MY YOUNG LOVER

a tired horse gallops up a mountain in the sad night wind
a spring meanders lonely in one corner of the sky
you, sweet breath of a time uncorked
what memory can I hold on to—what flowing hair, parted in two

a young squirrel stakes its fate on a strange mountain
and I, a forest bird, wings wearied with constant wounds
a scent of green grass cools ivory footprints
you, as blackboard & white chalk, our lives broken

a hundred butterflies swim home along the same course
a spring overflowing will have to leave its source
you, slender silk dress, more slender than a hill silhouette
O forest, how many years the trees waiting

you a pure and spotless thing in my dust-filled life
call me back to see the simple sunlight
you, just coming of age, your love a lure of waterfalls
pity me, a horse astray, cut off from the herd

Translations by Kevin Bowen and Nguyen Ba Chung

3045. TONKIN — Baie d'Along - Rade du Crapaud

Collection P. Dieulefils, Photographe, 53, rue Jules Ferry à Hanoi

from *dust and conscience*
(book of the familiar) ———————————————————————

ENDINGS

**

every word of every image is a step towards the end this urgency dictates that the sentence as we know it no longer an option grammar is obsolete stories once told in detailed chapters have been reduced to a noun and a verb the father dies the lover leaves in search of his own ending perhaps now the writing can finally begin

**

when looking for my father's grave site we asked that it be beneath a tree in a lifetime of seeking refuge from country and language and life itself he would have wanted it this way

**

that love could stem from the most remote corners of our imagination this is how things are and not how it could or should be that is to say it is not enough that a fruit can be ugly but to also have it be pickled for added sourness this is beyond the cruelest cruelty that is to say this is a story devoid of morals it can be told in the breath of a sentence the span of a lifetime that discretion is left to the one telling the story

**

i am reverting to that voice not capable of telling stories in place of the narrative that voice takes on a child's declarative i am the father i am the son i am the lover i am i am the voice that existed before there were stories stories for the telling the voice that speaks in cryptic tongues the voice that insists on saying i love you and hearing it as i you love

**

to end without ending on this preposition really i've tried to no avail for translated i am considered not whole of fragments and shards translated i am a shadow of

A Day in the Life

Peter slams the driver's side door and storms toward the liquor store, mad about Junior calling him a beer gopher. "Don't walk away mad, just walk away!" June yells out the window after him, laughing. Sitting in the back seat, Tuna and I smile at each other, shaking our heads. There's never peace between those two.

Then Tuna's smile leaks into a grimace. I know I have the same look even before I follow his eyes to the barrel of a nickel-plated revolver pointing in the driver's side window: a rival gang member. We must be slipping. Reflecting off the barrel, a neon Budweiser sign flickers from a bad connection, like the rhythm of my heartbeat. *This Bud's not for me,* I pray and look at the inside of my coffin: a two-door, hatch-back Datsun. The barrel nods. "Remember me?" says Nickel-plate, then June explodes out of the passenger-side door as a white flash floods the inside of the car.

"Boom!" I bolt out of bed, kneeing the metal locker inches above my legs. Cursing my neighbor for slamming his cell door, I lay back down resigned. Escape in dreams is as futile as escape in reality—five gun towers and twenty-foot-high walls are my daily reminders of that truth.

I soak in my surroundings as the last images of the street fade. My cell: two beds, one on top of the other, a sink, a shitter, and two lockers—all inside a space eleven feet long, four and a half feet wide, and eight feet high. I crawl off the top bunk in the lifeless, gray twilight and get ready for work.

While I'm brushing my teeth, a nasal, female keen begins its daily, drawn-out announcement: *North Block inmates have ten minutes to exit their cells and get to work or face the consequences.* If given only one wish made good at that moment, a wish for a muzzle on the P.A.-system banshee would beat out a wish for a parole date. I grab my Walkman and a Neruda book and exit the cell as my cell-mate enters. My cellie greets me with a smile and a "Good morning." I give a weak grunt and leave. I understand married couples have mornings when their partners' presence is sickening. You can imagine how prisoners forced to live with each other must feel. Ducking and dodging the mental patients who double as prisoners—men who are still drowsy with last night's psych meds—I make my way out of the musty housing unit.

As I walk up and out of the dungeon, the slate-gray, overcast sky reminds me of climbing out of the Datsun eleven years ago. That day anger, frustration, and, mostly, fear wrapped itself around a cold ball of lead in the pit of my stomach. If Peter hadn't come out of the liquor store shooting, who knows what would've happened. As it was, Nickel-plate retreated behind a car, shot back at Peter, and disappeared around some bushes, hitting nothing but the liquor store. On my way home that night, I promised myself two things: make Nickel-plate regret not killing me, and never again get caught in such a helpless position. I should've known that by exacting vengeance on him, I would find myself in yet another helpless position—indefinitely. But instead of the back seat of a parked car and a drawn .357 Magnum, it's now a recreational yard and five sniper rifles.

Three steps outside the housing unit, two guards are checking IDs, laundry bags, inmates' destinations, anything and everything they want. They are yard cops and my immediate bosses. My job mainly consists of typing write-ups: records of rule violations by inmates. Since I am one of three clerks, my work load is minimal. The majority of the day I spend reading, writing, exercising—doing things that benefit me and not my oppressors, which is the main reason I vied for this job. There is only one drawback. In typing a write-up, I'm technically assisting in lengthening a prisoner's incarceration, a fact I abhor and struggle with daily.

My bosses are in the middle of a joke as I check in: "You see the look on his face when I told him to get naked?!" This is a tactic used to intimidate prisoners deemed to have too much attitude. The official reason for the unclothed-body search is that the prisoner seemed suspicious, but the truth is, the guards didn't like seeing the anger and frustration on his face when he was ordered to let his possessions be searched.

The guards smile at me and I return the same. My smile, however, is tempered with the knowledge that the unfortunate prisoner could've been me if I wasn't their clerk. Between laughs, the taller of the two says the Squad has a write-up for me, then hands me a paper bag. The Squad is California Department of Corrections' CIA, FBI, and DEA all rolled up in one. He winks and says, "Merry Christmas." The bag is filled with items from the commissary that were confiscated from the naked prisoner: tobacco and coffee. He didn't have a receipt to prove he purchased the goods. I reply with a hollow "Thank you" and head toward the office area, holding the bag and feeling like the driver of a getaway car after a robbery.

A few moments later, I pass another checkpoint. A guard is harassing an inmate for smoking in a designated smoke-free zone. His master-speaking-to-slave tone shifts to dog-in-heat-seeking-relief when a nurse walks by, heading to the infirmary and smoking a cigarette. Just as quickly, he is back playing the overseer speaking to the field hand. *Ya know smokin da masta's crops illega in dees here parts.*

I round a bend and walk by the Adjustment Center, which is on my right and is better known as the AC. It is a squat block of a building decorated with barred windows. The AC houses a hundred of California's most infamous prisoners and has a hundred cells and four miniature yards: the entire world for these prisoners. I don't know what kind of adjustments occur in the center, but the few prisoners who exit its gates are often headed to the infirmary, if not the morgue.

To my left are four prison chapels: Muslim, Jewish, Protestant, and Catholic. These neat, white-painted buildings stand together facing the AC, looking like spectators at a lynching. I've always found the proximity of these buildings symbolic. Now if I can only figure out who's praying for whom. Is society praying for the individual who has failed so miserably, or is it the other way around?

Through two swinging doors, I walk to a heated office where inmate clerks are busy typing. I sit down at my word processor, situated in the corner of the room, and scan the handwritten charge: *possession of heroin*. The hapless addict is facing an extra three months.

I put on my Walkman and begin transferring the handwritten text onto forms specific to the write-up charge. I'm hoping the music will take my mind off my part in giving another prisoner more time. It never helps. After every correction I make and every word I type, I become more and more ill. It's as if I've swallowed something abominable. Worse: poison. Yes, I am killing myself. Every time I partake in this feast, where the powerful eat the helpless, a part of me dies. I feel sorry for the nearby clerks, who must see my agonized countenance. I glance up and see my pain on all their faces.

The write-up completed, I exit the office and head around a bend and down a slope to the Squad's office. Climbing five steps, I press a buzzer and wait. A moment later, a Nazi stormtrooper appears in a CDC jumpsuit, collects my folder, and sends me off with an unholy grin. I now know how Dante felt leaving the Ninth Circle.

At the bottom of the steps, I stop and hang my head in shame. To my left is the spot where George Jackson was murdered. I bow. I ask the Soledad brother to forgive a brother-in-spirit who's degraded himself by helping to lengthen another prisoner's incarceration. My daily tug-o-war between principles and comfort continues. *Am I compromising my beliefs? If I worked as a janitor in the prison infirmary or as a clerk in the warden's office, wouldn't I still be assisting the oppressors?* But comforts win yet again.

I head for the recreational yard to sweat the disgust off my body. A crisp wind bites through my state blues, carrying with it a message from the dead: *Don't be too hard on yourself, lil' brother. Your time will come and when it does, you'll make me proud.* I feel the shackles of imprisonment loosen on my limbs.

Floating by the first checkpoint on a euphoric high, I see a guard shooing away two homosexual prisoners as if they're mangy mutts who'd gotten too close to him. My body feels like a dead weight once again. Descending two flights of stairs to the yard, I find a vacant picnic table and take off my denim uniform, all the while thinking that only flies and their offspring have picnics here.

Wearing sweat pants that I'd had on under my jeans, I run. I run from guilt. I run from reality. I run to escape. Thirty minutes later, I am on all fours, almost retching from exhaustion. The taste of shame a little less sharp in my mouth, I grab a seat on a bench and watch as demons chase other prisoners around the quarter-mile track.

My mind wanders. I hitch a ride with clouds drifting overhead. I see myself lying on their cottony softness, being transported to better times: I am in the uppermost compartment of a linen closet. Hiding behind sheets and towels, I find solace in the fragrance of washed laundry and darkness.

A booming voice over the P.A. system pulls me away from my childhood refuge. The yard is closed. I get dressed and shuffle back to the stairs with the rest of the herd, wondering if I will ever find peace in darkness again. At the top of the stairs, I stop.

"Escooooort!" Death in handcuffs is flanked by flak-jacketed badges. I turn away from the condemned man and face the wall, a mirror image of the prisoners around me. I look to my left and see that a young Hispanic man with tattoos adorning his neck and face is reading his life line in the cracks on the wall. To my right, a long-haired, bearded white man, who reminds me of a short Jesus, is eyeing the ground, drooling for a chance to pick up the cigarette butts. I hand Jesus the brown bag filled with the loot that I've been carrying. He warily peeks inside, then hugs the bag to his chest as if all his earthly possessions are contained in it. I wonder what I look like in their eyes. They probably see what I see every morning in my pocket-sized mirror toothpasted to the wall: my father, a veteran who lost his country, and his dreams.

After a decade of incarceration, I still don't understand the logic of having to turn away from death-row prisoners who are escorted from one part of the prison to another. Shifting slightly, I see the condemned man being led to the law library around the next corner, holding his legal work in hands shackled behind his back. There is a disciplined calmness in his walk and demeanor that triggers my memory. I saw the same aura surrounding Buddhist monks in my homeland—right before they set themselves on fire. Maybe the administrators don't want us other inmates to see the indestructible human spirit on their faces because the chamber, chair, or needle is useless against such an opponent. "Escooooort!" Zombies scatter. Or maybe the administrators don't want the condemned to see our faces. Since we are the ones who look like the walking dead, the misery of the condemned would be diluted by the knowledge that we're all damned when we're imprisoned.

Turning away from the burning monk, I melt into the stream of men heading back to the housing unit. The smell of cooking meat is heavy in the air—tonight's dinner. I taste bile in my mouth. Ahead, the six-abreast herd of men is bottlenecked at a doorway one and a half men wide. After a few minutes, I enter a bustling morgue.

Five tiers and two hundred and ten cells—each originally built to hold one man but now accommodating two—stare me in the face. I'm reminded of a giant beehive where death has made his home. I follow the inching flow of rush-hour traffic around a corner and see the same monster: another five tiers and two hundred and ten cells. Finally, on the two-foot-wide stair that I'm sure was a fire escape in a prior life, I ascend in single file, along with the other hundred-plus worker bees.

There are men standing in front of their cells, some talking seriously, some laughing. Others are panhandling door to door for a fix of coffee or tobacco; many are showering, and many are still dreaming in a Thorazine-influenced sleepwalk. The buzzing of eight hundred men is almost insanity-inducing. I can understand why every so often a new booty climbs the stairs to the fifth tier and, instead of stopping, continues over the railing, his scream lost in the cacophony.

When my father and our family joined the crowd at the U.S. embassy's gates during South Viet Nam's collapse in 1975, I wonder if in his wildest nightmare he imagined a future like this for his son. I wonder if he believes that by cheating his fate—sure imprisonment for his anticommunist views—he may have angered the gods to such a degree that fate, crawling out of the shadows of time, finds my flesh much sweeter. I try to imagine what his life would've been like if he had stayed in Viet Nam. Could it be much worse than my life now? I snort and laugh. After twenty-five years of Americanization, I still can't shake my cultural superstitions.

On the narrow tier, I have to squeeze by two youngsters in deep conversation. "I would die for you, homeboy!" I hear one say to the other. Gangster bonding. Words I lived by for much of my life. In hindsight, I recognize what a hollow truth that was. It's not that I wasn't willing to die for my homies—I was; and, in a sense, by serving a life sentence for killing a rival gang member who threatened them—I am. The hollowness about it was that I was hollow. Under my silent and fearless exterior, which I mastered by practicing the philosophy that men are like rocks—hard and emotionless—I was empty inside. It was as if a chain hung around my neck with a heavy medallion of nothingness attached to it. And instead of the chain resting on my chest, it sunk into my chest cavity, banging into ribs and organs, rattling with my every breath. I have an impulse to correct the young Al Capone: *I would endure nothingness for you, homeboy!* But I don't. Gangster etiquette.

Once in my cell, I flip on the radio. As I peel down and get ready for my shower, I hear there's been another school shooting. I don't know if I'm more disgusted with the waste of human life or with the media circus sure to come afterwards. Probably the latter. The greater waste is when death becomes entertainment for the living. I can already hear the grave voice of a commentator asking, "How can we as a community not see the signs that lead up to such a tragedy?" They should've used their ears instead of their eyes. The *clink, clink, clink* of chain and nothingness against ribs is unmistakable. Even under the maddening din of blaring speakers, slamming gates, screaming whistles and alarms, I can still recognize its hollow ring. It's most noticeable at night, when I'm counting stars on a moonless ceiling and everyone's asleep. The ringing reminds me of chimes on the front porch of my childhood home. Coming home from elementary school, I would find the house empty. And no matter where I went in the house, even the farthest bedroom, I would hear those chimes ring. I'd even go into the bathroom and close the door, but still I would hear those chimes. After a few years, the ringing became part of me.

Along the tier and down a flight of steps and I'm at the watering hole. It's crowded: twenty-eight showerheads for eight hundred men. Fourteen showerheads are reserved for blacks, the other half for the rest of the population. The Old South is alive and well in California prisons. C&D air is blowing through a door twenty feet away, and puddles of foul water lie in wait on the ground: a fungus minefield. How many more of these showers must I endure to get clean? I hold my breath and submerge myself in inhumanity.

I get in and come out quickly, but not quickly enough. Someone has mistaken the towel and boxers that I hung up for his own. I walk back to my cell naked and wet. While I'm toweling off in the cell, my name is blared through the loudspeaker. I have visitors. I forgot that this is the time of month my parents pay their respects. My family has two altars for paying homage to dead family members: one is on the mantel above the fireplace of our home; the other is in the visiting room at my prison.

Mom and Dad are sitting at a knee-high table, hunched over vending-machine food. They seem to be praying like they do at home in front of the fireplace, bowing to pictures of my grandparents and making food offerings. Instead of the sharp scent of incense, cheap perfume chokes the air. They greet me with smiles that fail to reach their eyes. We sit and my mom begins telling me about life being too hectic at her age; about trouble with the in-laws; about my nephew being old enough to walk and talk and ask why his uncle is in prison. I feel like a ghost hearing her thoughts as she kneels in front of the fireplace. Next to me, my dad sits silently, eyeing the people around us who remind him of dead Americans he once knew.

Two hours pass quickly. Visiting hours are over. We get up and my mom starts to cry. I hug her and am still amazed that her head only reaches my sternum. I wonder how a woman of her small stature can carry such enormous loads of suffering. She fled her homeland to save her husband from imprisonment, only to find imprisonment waiting for her son in America. I stroke her trembling back, trying to soften her pain, remembering the way she used to comfort me as a child: humming my favorite lullaby while passing her gentle hand through my hair. I hear the same lullaby and realize I'm humming it to her. She looks up at me with tired eyes in tears, telling me that she's ready for her picture to be placed on our mantel, but that she holds off eternal peace until the return of her son.

My dad pats me on the back and repeats, "Hang in there. Hang in there." I look into his eyes and get the feeling that even though he's looking at me, he's addressing himself. It's as if he believes that the life sentence I'm now serving should be his and that if he survives his guilty conscience, then I will survive my sentence. I pull away and disappear in a sea of tears and farewells. In the strip-out area, I wait in line to let a stranger look into my body cavities.

Back in my cell, I take my mind off my problems by reading a book by Neruda. *Blood has fingers and it opens tunnels underneath the earth.* How did a Chilean poet describe an experience that only a Viet Cong could know? Pondering yet another of life's ironies, I let Pablo's words, the clinking chimes, and the occasional toilet flushing, whisper me to sleep.

I'm in the back seat of a parked car. It's not a Datsun but a military jeep. There is no laughter, although Peter, June, and Tuna are in their usual places. Instead of leather jackets and dress slacks, we're wearing green military fatigues. A bead of sweat slithers down the back of my neck and then down my spine, leaving goose bumps in its wake. There is fear in the air that is thicker than the sticky heat surrounding everything. This is not California. I'm wondering why Peter isn't leaving to buy beer when I realize we're not at a liquor store but a road block. I see a group of armed Vietnamese soldiers, dressed in military fatigues different from ours, approach our jeep. Something is definitely not right here, yet everything is eerily familiar. My boys file out of the jeep, and I'm about to do the same when the barrel of an AK-47 pounds my chest, knocking me backwards onto the seat. The barrel eases into the driver's side window and nods. *Remember me?* The words do not come from human lips. I have a picture of something that crawls on its belly and lives in shadows. In a voice not my own and filled with resignation, I answer, *Yes.*

Boom! An intense, burning pain digs into my chest. I look down and see a smoking hole leaking blood and, next to it, a name tag. TU DO, it reads. My father's name. I look up and see my father's face staring back at me in the rearview mirror. I gag.

Bolting out of bed, I knee my locker and grab my throat, not wanting to swallow my tongue. On the P.A. system, a nasal female voice is in the middle of a drawn-out threat.

12. SAIGON — Jardin botanique - La pergola

A Strange Letter

My name is Linh Dinh and I am American. (At least that's what my passport says.) My wife's name is Diem Bui and she is not. (At least not yet.) We got married on 24 December 2000 in Saigon, the city of my birth.

I am American insofar as I read the box scores every morning, eat French fries on a regular basis, know that Buster Keaton is a genius. I am Vietnamese insofar as I have black hair, yellow skin, and a Napoleon complex.

A Vietnamese American is a special breed in Viet Nam. Unlike an American American, he is not a total alien. He brings news from the promised land and, sometimes, is even a bridge to it.

Soon after our wedding, my wife received a strange letter from a distant cousin, someone she had not seen or talked to for more than a decade. The writer of this letter was a twenty-three-year-old woman:

Beloved Diem!
How are you? I am so happy for you. You are very lucky.
On the occasion of your wedding, I want to send you and your husband my deepest and most sincere wishes for your future happiness.
My mother is doing fine. I'm still in school. I'm getting rather fat and so have been on a diet.
You haven't been back to Can Tho in a long time. Perhaps you don't even remember me. I still have very fond memories of your visit in 1989. I was so happy to see you because I am the only girl in my family. Even back then you were very fashionably dressed. Do you remember? The two of us went all over Can Tho. We ate roasted corn; you took me to school, helped me with my homework. We rented Hong Kong videos and stayed up until two in the morning. Then we fried up some duck eggs with scallions. Do you remember?
I was very reluctant to send you this letter. I was afraid you would misunderstand my intentions. Why haven't I been in touch? Why am I getting in touch with you now? Now that you have a rich husband.
My beloved Diem, I was only a kid before, distracted by school and play, and did not know a thing about writing letters. I also did not have your address. Aunt Tam never gave me your phone number. I didn't even know you

had a phone. All I knew was that you live by the Phu Lam Bridge in Saigon. How can I send a letter to a bridge? *(Ha! Ha! Ha!)*

But when you sent Aunt Tam your wedding photos, I finally got your address. My first thought was that you are truly a lucky girl! I love you very much. I'm not trying to suck up to you now that you have a rich husband. That's not how I live; I don't chase after money. We have a saying down this way: Don't let your conscience bite you in the ass!

It's true that my family is very poor now. But a torn shirt need not stink. Just because you're poor doesn't mean you have to suck up to anyone.

If only I were as lucky as you, how happy I'd be. I have dreamt of coming to America since I was ten, maybe earlier, but this lifelong dream has brought me nothing but disappointment. Now I don't think about it anymore. My mother used to be good friends with a woman who lives in Miami, a city just outside New York. One time she came by to show us pictures of her son, someone roughly my age. She even let me keep some of these pictures. I gave her some pictures in return. We all thought this woman meant something by it, that she had good intentions, but she never followed up. Why did she tease us like that? I even broke up with my boyfriend to prepare for a new life.

Maybe her son didn't think I was attractive enough. Or maybe I had on the wrong clothes. Us country girls really don't know how to dress. But the truth is, and don't laugh when I tell you this, I didn't think her son was all that good looking either. He was rather a dork. To hell with him!

I only wanted to come to America so I could help my mother out by sending money home each month.

To make a long story short: I'm just not a lucky girl. Not at all like you. But why am I boring you with my sad story? I better shut up before I put you to sleep! Seeing you so happy makes me a little happier.

With much love to you.

Your lost cousin,
Tran Tu Ngoc

I asked my wife about Tran Tu Ngoc and was told that her family deals in electronics. They have a four-story house, and she has vacationed in six different countries.

Speaking of electronics, during my twenty-four years in the U.S., I never owned a television, a CD player, a boombox, or an air conditioner. I never had a checking account. The only car I've ever bought was a used Mustang II, which was stolen from me in less than a year.

Once I went to a supermarket and paid for a packet of Ramen Pride with 28 pennies.

Another time I paid for a can of Spam with 159 pennies.

I waited until there was no one around before I went to the cash register, but as I counted out my pennies for the grinning cashier—as I formed for her 16 mounds of nearly worthless currency, minted merely to decorate the bottoms of shopping-mall fountains—a long line grew behind me.

Once, in the cheapest bar in Philadelphia, I tried to pay for a mug of Rolling Rock with 60 pennies and was told to get the fuck out.

"You have to take this! It's real money."

"Get the fuck out of here!"

This is the implied P.S. to the strange letter: Your husband must have a Vietnamese American friend who might be interested in a country girl like me.

41. - HANOI. - La Pagode du Grand Bouddha

The Long Road Home: Exile, Self-Recognition, and Reconstruction

A thousand years enslaved by China
A hundred years trampled by France
Twenty years of civil war day by day
Our mother's inheritance: a forest of dried bones
Our mother's inheritance: a mountain of endless graves

"Mother's Inheritance," Trinh Cong Son

A Call to Conscience

During the entire Vietnamese-American War, Trinh Cong Son was the bard who perhaps most powerfully, most eloquently, most persistently, and most successfully put into song the sense of unspeakable tragedy that befell ordinary Vietnamese people, without any regard for geography or politics. All sides were intent on victory. Few took note, or were allowed to take note, of what the war did to the mass of people at the bottom rung of society. Trinh Cong Son's songs had an incomparable appeal to all, Northern as well as Southern, urban as well as rural, rich as well as poor. For that reason, he was condemned by politicians of all stripes. To favor the continuation of the war—as the politicians all did—one had to avert one's eyes from what was happening to the people, the land, and the culture. Trinh Cong Son could not do that.

The war demanded that people take sides. In the South, Trinh Cong Son and a few others always skirted the edges; most writers in the South, however—whether willingly or pushed by the exigencies of circumstances —felt compelled to choose sides. In the North, support among the writers for the leadership and against the Americans was mostly unquestioned and unquestionable. When Viet Nam was unified in 1975, South Vietnamese writers who had sided against the North and who were still in the country were sent to "study camps" for reeducation and socialist reorientation. Only a few could make the adjustment to life under communism. The great majority had to give up the pen, instead making a meager living doing all manner of odd jobs. Hundreds chose to risk their lives and go into exile, leaving their fate in the hands of the ocean winds and waves.

The year 1979 marked the beginning of a dramatic phase in the development of Vietnamese diasporic literature. The sudden arrival of a massive number of "boat people" in the United States caused a change in the thinking of the exiled writers who had arrived earlier. They had been inward looking and had felt cut off from their home country. From the writers who had just escaped, however, they learned of the terrible conditions there. First-wave writers were challenged by stories of the brutality, hunger, and lack of freedom that drove second-wave refugees to brave the sea, survive pirate attacks, and languish in refugee camps, and they transformed their loneliness to make it serve a new mission. They felt they were the only ones left who could keep alive the Viet Nam they had known and loved, albeit in memory, and who could transmit it to the next generation. This awakened the desire to establish a diasporic literature—one that would defend and preserve the true Vietnamese cultural heritage. A number of literary magazines and reviews began to appear in this period, laying the foundation for the exile literature to come. Mai Thao, the indisputable dean of South Viet Nam literary society, arrived in the States in 1978, and he started the first prestigious émigré literary journal in July 1982. His words on that occasion captured the missionary fervor of the time:

> To me, the love of our great native land and the compassion towards her greatest tragedy should always be the lasting and glorious beacon for all literary activities. And there should exist no other guiding principle.

Between 1986 and 1989, diasporic literature came into full bloom. Nguyen Mong Giac calls this the golden period. The sense of the exile community as the center of resistance to the communist government, and as the only carrier of hope for the masses inside Viet Nam, was at its most intense. But underneath this fervor, a crack had already appeared. December 1986 marked the beginning of the Vietnamese government's policy of Doi Moi (Renovation). This policy of apparent reform and loosening of censorship caused the exile literary community to split into two camps. Believing that the whole thing was a ruse to trick the unwary, the conservative group, represented by *Lang Van* (Literary Circle) and local community weeklies, called for heightened vigilance. The moderate wing, however, welcomed Doi Moi changes and adopted a more open-minded, wait-and-see attitude.

The decade of the nineties proved problematic. The split widened, and today there is still no consensus in the community. While the conservative group, backed by a flood of newly arrived H.O. parolees, hardened its militant anticommunist stand, the moderate wing moved in the other direction: towards dialogue. (H.O. is a program that allowed former South Vietnamese officers and administrators to be released from reeducation camps and sent to the States.) Under the editorship of Khanh Truong, an ex-paratrooper, the journal *Hop Luu* (Confluence) appeared in October 1991 with the proclaimed objective of publishing works by writers both inside and outside Viet Nam. Its policy was to abandon the path of enmity and division in favor of a "confluence," joining the best of the culture with the people's interests. In June 1992, *Tram Con* (A Hundred Children) appeared in Montreal, Canada, under the editorship of Tran Sa and took a similar stand. Both were denounced by *Lang Van* as propaganda pieces for Ha Noi. Deep, unhealed wounds left over from the protracted war were reopened in these conflicts. For some, Doi Moi presented the occasion for a redefinition of the diasporic community's anticommunist stand against the homeland; for others, it necessitated a further hardening of that stand. Quickly joining the ranks of community organizers, many H.O. newcomers advocated an absolute prohibition on all contact with Viet Nam: "no visits, no remittance, no cooperation." Khanh Truong, Nguyen Mong Giac, and Nguyen Xuan Hoang—the editors-in-chief of the top three exile literary journals— were, at one time or another, attacked in local community newspapers as being procommunist.

In October 2000, Hoang Ngoc Hien, a well-known and highly respected critic in Viet Nam, came to the U.S. to study diasporic literature for six months. He was followed in March 2001 by Nguyen Hue Chi, an internationally known scholar of classical and modern Vietnamese literature and philosophy. Both traveled widely in the States and met prominent exile writers living in Texas, the District of Columbia, and California. For the first time, frank and genuine conversations could take place between exile and homeland writers. Interestingly, they found that they had things in common, the most notable one being the pressure to conform. While the top literary journals abroad—*Van Hoc* (Literary Study), *Hop Luu* (Confluence), and *Tho* (Poetry)—published widely acclaimed articles by Hoang Ngoc Hien and Nguyen Hue Chi, the conservative group denounced both men as "high-ranking" communist officials whose mission was to "rewrite the history of the refugees." Their visit to the U.S. was labeled part of "the communist plot to infiltrate the exile community."

This conflict highlights the deepening polarization of the overseas Vietnamese community. With the gradual integration of Viet Nam into the world community, the militant anticommunist wing finds itself increasingly threatened. Ironically, it sees everything with a political slant and labels anyone who deviates from its dogmas the enemy—a perception very much like the one it accuses its adversary as having. Some exile writers wryly dismiss the conflict as theater of the absurd.

To search for a deeper explanation of Mai Thao's passionate call to conscience and of the virulent opposition to it, we must go back in time.

A Clash of Worlds and Worldviews

Vo Phien, one of the most eminent South Vietnamese writers in exile, observed in his *Twenty Years of South Viet Nam Literature, 1954–1975: An Overview* that the figure of the peasant is noticeably missing in South Vietnamese literature in those decades.

Except for a few cases, the peasant, if he exists as a character at all, is a stick figure, devoid of any substance and relevance. This is a startling observation considering the fact that over eighty percent of South Vietnamese were peasants at the time.

How can we explain this remarkable state of affairs? How could the literature of South Viet Nam reflect the thoughts and concerns of a mere twenty percent of the population—those who lived securely in the city, beyond the storm of shellings and bombings and the ever-present threat of bullets whizzing by? Saigon and many other cities in South Viet Nam at that time existed like islands of peace and comfort in a sea of fires, from which they turned their eyes. Protected by U.S. military power and supported by generous U.S. aid, these cities had the appearance of wealthy first-world enclaves in a land of third-world poverty and suffering. For the most part, urban writers concerned themselves with problems more appropriate to a country not at war, or at least not fighting for its survival. Unlike their compatriots in the countryside, these writers never had their lives threatened. They may not have approved of communism, but it was a rather abstract specter to them and, in point of fact, only tangentially impinged upon their daily existence; in contrast, the corruption of the government and the debasement and destruction of the nation's cultural values by the presence of a massive foreign army were apparent and immediate. In many ways, the urban writers were trapped by a history not of their own choosing: they could neither wholeheartedly support those who claimed to fight in their names, nor could they completely disassociate themselves. They could not leave the security of the city to join the guerrilla forces in the jungle, nor could they categorically reject and condemn those who did, for no one could deny the zeal, dedication, and self-sacrifice of the other side or the corruption within their own. As unruly and difficult to govern as ever, South Viet Nam thus allowed them a measure of nonconformity and doubt that was absent in the North, and that remained absent after 1975.

Against this first-world luxury of Hamlet-like irresolution, self-questioning, and existential self-doubt stood the self-affirming determination of those who toiled in the back-breaking rice fields, lived in underground tunnels, and faced capture or annihilation every day—with no foreign air power or allied troops ready to spring to their rescue. A South Vietnamese politician or general could live in opulence in a French-built villa and enjoy all the conveniences of the first world, including several servants to run errands for him. In contrast, a general or political commissar of the liberation forces lived deep in the forest, in a hut or underground tunnel, and could, along with his troops, go hungry for months. He had no first-world trappings: no TV, no cars, no news about life in the first world. His heart was burning with a single desire: to keep his troops alive, or at least slow their decimation for as long as possible. He experienced over and over the pain of seeing his units face annihilation by B-52 carpet bombings, napalm attacks, offshore naval bombardments, and firebase artillery bar-rages. He believed the source of all his suffering, and the suffering of his fel-low villagers, lay at the doorstep of the South Vietnamese and their Amer-ican "masters," who lived comfortably behind the security zones ringing the cities. Because the liberation forces had agents in the highest reaches of the South Vietnamese government, generals living in the jungles knew about South Viet Nam's subordinate relationship in a way that most of its citizens could not. Those who did would never publicly admit it—an ironic example of Lao Tse's saying "Those who know do not speak; those who speak do not know."

After the war, in the period from 1975 to 1986, when the country went into steep economic decline, it was a hellish fall for most people in the South, but particularly for those who lived in the city. In contrast, for those who had survived constant hunger and want in the jungle during the war, such subsistence living was preferable to what they had endured. The resulting clash was therefore not simply of ideologies, but of two altogether different worlds in which the very meaning of language was in dispute. In one world, to be able to live in peace, to have food to eat (regardless of how simple or meager) and clothes to wear, and to rest one's head in an above-ground shelter were achievements and were among the sweet freedoms enjoyed by those who had survived. In the other world, those who had lived in relative comfort were now preoccupied with defeat and the loss of those individual freedoms that had come with life in a modern urban society.

With all their existential ambivalence, South Vietnamese writers who remained in the country after 1975 were treated as nonconformists and therefore potential threats to the new socialist vision, which had confor-mity as one of its distinguishing marks. Many writers didn't flee when Saigon collapsed, believing that unification would bring peace, forgiveness, and a willingness to have everyone join efforts to rebuild a shattered coun-try. That hope was quickly dashed. Their experiences in the reeducation camps—where they were treated not as individuals trapped by circum-stances, but as willing collaborators and traitorous agents of the imperial-ists—left a wounding and indelible mark on them. From the well of that bitter memory springs forth the literature of overseas Vietnamese today, which is, in many aspects, a continuation and extension of the literature of South Viet Nam before 1975.

Cultural Discontinuities

Viet Nam's cultural clashes have a deeper history, originating in the subterranean segmentation of the culture that began in the fifteenth century, expanded considerably by the late nineteenth cen-tury, and became cast in concrete by the late twentieth century.

Today there may be a unified country called Viet Nam, with a popula-tion of seventy-eight million inside its borders and over two million in exile overseas; but in actuality, there are many "little Viet Nams"—culturally, religiously, and politically—which were brought into being, nurtured, and kept separate in the last century by various political forces, internal and external. Three periods of major cultural disruptions and discontinuities are responsible for the creation of these deeply divided "little Viet Nams."

In *The Birth of Vietnam*, scholar Keith Taylor traces the origin of the country back to the third century B.C.E. However, Viet Nam came into being as a powerful state under the Ly Tran dynasties, which lasted from the eleventh to the fifteenth centuries. The extraordinary feats of repulsing three successive Mongolian invasions, unifying the native culture, centralizing the state administration, and, above all, encouraging the flowering of literature are the legacies of this period. Integral to these events was the profound role played by a unique Way called Tam Giao Dong Nguyen, or the One Sourced Triple Teaching, which united Buddhism, Confucianism, and Taoism with native beliefs. Many rulers were not just kings but also Zen masters, leading the nation with a degree of tolerance, compassion, and creativity that was unprecedented in Vietnamese history.

The first discontinuity occurred at the beginning of the fifteenth century. Following the Chinese administrative model, the Le dynasty promoted Confucianism as the state doctrine in order to strengthen its absolute reach. Buddhist monks, no longer welcome in the corridor of power, returned to the village and carried on their tradition among the peasantry. The king ruled with the help of his mandarinate, whose scholars could only be appointed after passing examinations based on the Four Books and the Five Classics of Confucianism. With time, the national intellectual temper became much more dogmatic and less tolerant. The atmosphere of freedom, inclusiveness, and tolerance that had prevailed under the influence of Buddhism dissipated, leading to civil war among the Mac, the Trinh, and the Nguyen during the sixteenth to the eighteenth centuries.

In his article "Culture As a Motive for Development," Nguyen Hue Chi describes two governing models in this era of Vietnamese history. The first was composed of the pluralistic *(da nguyen)*, freewheeling *(tu do thoai mai)*, and syncretic *(dung hop)* dynasties of Ly Tran, wherein Buddhism, Confucianism, and Taoism coexisted and flowered. The second was composed of the monophilosophical (Confucianism only), monopolistic *(doc quyen)*, and unnatural *(phi tu nhien)* regime under Le Thanh Tong. He considers the latter, which was able to rise to eminence—but only for a short time—to be at odds with native Vietnamese culture, and he concludes, "Vietnamese culture both in the past and in the present has always thrown into the dustbin quietly and in due time, though it may take a long while but always inexorably, phenomena that deviate from its law." Nevertheless, the competition between these two governing models created the first period of cultural disruption.

The second cultural disruption began as a result of the signing of the

Patenôtre Accord in 1884, marking the loss of Vietnamese sovereignty and the start of eighty years of French colonialism. During this period, all revolts by scholars failed, crushed repeatedly and brutally by French troops and their Vietnamese allies. These failures led to prolonged national self-doubt about the value of Viet Nam's cultural heritage. Not only Buddhism but Confucianism as well seemed unable to offer a solution to this national crisis. And as French was the official language of the colonial adminis-tration and the school system, a new generation of young Vietnamese attempted to seek ways to regain independence through Western teachings; in doing so, they gave up hope in the resources of their traditional culture, creating a schism between the old and the new. In strengthening the posi-tion of Catholicism, seeing it as a reliant partner in maintaining colonial order, France created another state within a state, further fragmenting the culture. This led to the Van Than (Scholars') Revolt, in which Vietnamese Catholics and Vietnamese rebels, led by the scholars, massacred one another. Traditional Vietnamese culture, Western teaching, and Catholi-cism became three separate islands, each with its own worldview, its own interpretation of the past, its own hope for the future, and its own sense of patriotism. They were like three ships passing in the night in a sea that had once been a unified Viet Nam.

With the victory in Dien Bien Phu, communism triumphed, and as a result could claim that its ideology was the only governing model capable of erasing the stain of eighty years of colonialism. Flush with self-confi-dence and a sincere and unshakable belief in the future, the communist leadership proceeded to weaken the hold of the old culture, seeing it as an impediment to social progress and thereby fostering the third discontinuity in Vietnamese history. In response to the international temper of the time, Catholicism and communism became the two most bitter adversaries. More than seven hundred thousand Catholics left North Viet Nam to go south, joining the crusade against "godless" communism. Never in Viet-namese history was there such a deep rift in the body politic. Culturally, a unified Viet Nam no longer existed. The country had become a miniature battleground of what Samuel Huntington called the "clash of civiliza-tions."

The Vietnamese-American War deepened this rift to an unprecedented degree, exasperating the differences among the many other "little Viet Nams." The national temper of tolerance, compassion, and acceptance of different ideas found in Tam Giao Dong Nguyen, the Triple Teaching prevalent under the Ly Tran dynasties, took a heavy beating, and the ground became fertile for the planting of religious dogmatism, intolerance, and absolutism. A culture that has been drastically transformed too many times is in danger of losing its elasticity and its capacity to find a common ground. We can still see the effects of these cultural and historical transfor-mations in Viet Nam and in the exile community, although the new forces of integration, the impact of recent international contacts, and the revival of the genuine spirit of religion have restored some of the tolerance and unity of the Ly Tran era.

Self-Recognition and Reconstruction

A number of events that started in the 1990s have caused the exile literary community to do a serious reassessment. Foremost among these is the appearance of several world-class works from Viet Nam: for example, Nguyen Huy Thiep's short stories (especially "No King," "The Retired General," and "Our Village in Fond Memory"), Bao Ninh's "The Sorrow of War," Duong Thu Huong's "Paradise of the Blind," Pham Thi Hoai's "Messenger from Heaven," Nguyen Duy's "Distant Road," and, most recently, Bui Ngoc Tan's "Story of the Year 2000."

Clearly, a belief held by some in the exile community is no longer tenable: that writers in Viet Nam are all Communist Party hacks, that their writing has nothing to offer, and that the overseas literary community stands as the only hope for the continuation of an authentic Vietnamese literature—as Mai Thao passionately believed. The fact is that some of the most critical works about the dark side of socialism come not from the exile community but from those who grew up under it and live their lives in it. To paraphrase a common saying: those who experienced socialism through the postwar decade or the reeducation camps were perhaps exposed only to its skin; those who have grown up and been molded in it can speak about it from its marrow. After reading Bui Ngoc Tan's "Story of the Year 2000," Lam Chuong, a noted writer of Southern tales and former Ranger captain in the South Viet Nam Army, decided that he would no longer write about his experiences in the reeducation camp.

The second notable event to cause the exile community to reassess itself has been the success and influence of a number of overseas journals, especially Khanh Truong's *Hop Luu* (Confluence), Nguyen Mong Giac's *Van Hoc* (Literary Study), Nguyen Xuan Hoang's *Van* (Literature), and Khe Iem's *Tho* (Poetry). These journals publish works not only by overseas writers, but also by writers within Viet Nam—a policy roundly condemned by the more vocal and political wing of the overseas community as "collaborative" or, worse, "communist inspired." The editorial policies of these journals increasingly reflect a soft convergence—though by no means a unity—of views. *Hop Luu* and *Tho* have a sizable following in Viet Nam, though these two, like all the others, are banned there. *Hop Luu* is notable for its rich variety of highly literary fare, and *Tho* for its excellent translations of contemporary Western critical theories and discussion of trends, to which writers in Viet Nam rarely have access.

The gradual but steady strengthening of the more independent and inclusive views from within Viet Nam, as demonstrated recently by Nguyen Hue Chi's proposal for a new anthology of Vietnamese literature, is another trend that is bridging the schism between communities. He considers the literature of pre–1975 South Viet Nam and the literature of Vietnamese overseas to be indisputable parts of Vietnamese literature and feels that both must be included and treated seriously in any future anthology. This is not an idle proposal, for as chair of the department of classical and modern literature at the National Institute of Literature, Nguyen Hue Chi will be responsible for compiling a sizable number of volumes for this ground-breaking anthology.

The growing contact between the overseas community and the homeland via home visits and, even more critically, cultural exchanges is also breaking down the divisions created by past experiences and lingering memories of strife. Meanwhile, the younger diasporic generation is increasingly less interested in recounting the divisiveness between the home country and the exile community. Writers such as Barbara Tran, Christian Langworthy, Le Thi Diem Thuy, Mộng-Lan, Le Bi, Thuong Quan, and Khe Iem are more concerned with their dual identities in America than with issues related to the social and political ruptures of the past. Writers such as Linh Dinh, Do Kh., and Nguyen Qui Duc go one step further: they travel to Viet Nam again and again in search of an elusive connection to a world they could otherwise have only imagined through patches of shifting memory.

In addition, the growing numbers of younger writers like those just mentioned, together with the passing of a generation for whom the old schisms are important, pose a dilemma for exile writers. If their audience becomes mainly the people in Viet Nam, they will have to adjust to the political sea change that has occurred there. As the saying goes, "Politicians last but a while; the people endure forever." In any case, because the conservative wing of the overseas community opposes any visit to the homeland—its aim is the overthrow of the government in Viet Nam—a future literary audience is not even a blip on its political radar screen. And whenever any exchanges and contacts with Viet Nam take place, literary or otherwise, the conservative wing feels the need to exert a counterforce. Hence, its "take-no-prisoners" stratagem of protest.

In its fight to gain control of the soul and future direction of the exile community, the conservative wing wants to hold fast to the past and to extend the past indefinitely into the future. It remains uninformed of what's going on, not only in the literary community inside Viet Nam, but also among its own members. It is hardly in a position to build a path to the future. The moderate wing has left the past behind in its search for a future that is still open to change and possibility. This wing is composed of the best writers of the literary community overseas. It is well informed, not only about diasporic literature, but also about all the literary movements in Viet Nam. The tragedy of all this is that, just as South Viet Nam was once torn endlessly by factions, the exile community, despite twenty-five years of living in the most advanced and democratic country in the world, remains very much a South Viet Nam in microcosm. The wounds of war are deep and fresh for some. But more enmity and conflict will not heal them.

Cultural Convergences

> A thousand years enslaved by China
> A hundred years trampled by France
> Twenty years of civil war day by day
> Our mother's inheritance: a band of lost children
> Our mother's inheritance: a party of ingrates

It was out of unbearable pain over the suffering of his people that Trinh Cong Son wrote these words. What have we done to ourselves, to our people? In whose name do we have the right to commit these acts? What kind of children are we to have forgotten the way of our mother? What kind of descendants are we to have turned a blind eye towards the cultural treasure of the past, our mother's most precious inheritance? These song lyrics are not words of condemnation, but of pain and sadness. They are a call to achieve self-recognition, to become aware of what we have all done, of how far we have strayed from the roots of our cultural inheritance.

In a way we are fortunate to have these words for they represent the deepest passion of the culture in defense of life and compassion—in defense of the defenseless. The political fight might have to be fought, the ideologues will argue; but let us be aware of the terrible cost to be paid and the absence of vainglory in it. Words from Trinh Cong Son's songs seem to rise from the soil itself, cascading like wave after wave over the distant fields and creating an emotional space of such intensity that all arguments lose their hold except for those that advocate the need to alleviate the enormity of our pain.

Twenty-five years after the Vietnamese-American War ended, there is evidence that a cultural revival is steadily blooming in Viet Nam. Most informed people in Viet Nam understand that the socialist ethic has failed, that socialism has failed to create the new man fervently hoped for. The most trenchant analysis of society is offered not by those within the Party, but by those who have left it or come from the outside. The tradition of unflinching courage in the face of reality exemplified first by the old monks and scholars and later by the communists during the two Indochina wars is now exemplified by the ex-communists and today's religious leaders. Ready to risk their own lives, they make an attempt to remain true to the country's inheritance: an ancient, deeply humanistic culture. They have become exiles in their own home. Interestingly, as Viet Nam has made substantial progress in raising the living standard of its people, many issues that concerned the writers of South Viet Nam prior to 1975—the place of the free individual in society, the nature of government itself, and so forth—are resurfacing. In this regard, when Nguyen Mong Giac's *Song Con Mua Lu* (The Con River in the Season of Flood) was allowed to be reprinted in Viet Nam, many read it with quiet appreciation. *Ho Quy Ly*, which came out in Viet Nam in 2000, deals with similar subjects.

At the same time, Vietnamese writers overseas have finally been able to carve out a place in their adopted country. As the problem of basic survival has been resolved, they begin to face new and urgent questions about their identity and the degree of cultural homogenization that is possible or desirable. One of the characteristics of the literature of South Viet Nam prior to 1975—and, by extension, of the literature overseas today—was its spiritual seeking: a questioning of the individual's place not just in the world, but beyond it. This characteristic is demonstrated by the fact that every year in the U.S., France, and Australia, overseas Vietnamese writers publish dozens of popular titles on Buddhism, Taoism, Confucianism, the inner life, self-training, and the occult. In the socialist literature produced from 1945 to 1987, that aspect was conspicuously absent, as the socialist writer was concerned only with matters of the material world; anything else was idle daydreaming, if not downright superstition. But today we see that hundreds of titles on traditional philosophies have been published in Viet Nam and have garnered a wide readership. This revival could be traced to the publication of the two-thousand-page *Tho Van Ly Tran* (Poetry and Prose of the Ly Tran Dynasties), the first volume of which appeared in 1977.

These interests in matters spiritual—and, by extension, the proper roles of government, politics, community, and ideology—are upland springs and eddies that eventually become wide rivers leading to the sea. In the manifesto for *Hop Luu*, Khanh Truong foresaw the coming together of two rivers.

That is the beginning of the new journey: the tasks of critical social reconstruction on the one hand and self-recognition on the other; both contribute to the conception of a genuine future yet to be discovered. Vietnamese, whether living in exile or in the homeland, look forward to a peaceful, unified, democratic, and prosperous Viet Nam—something they deserve after the conflicts of the last century. Only in a centered mind free of hatred and illusion—about either past or future—can a genuinely critical and passionate literature come forth.

> I return, a mysterious dream
> Like a child looking for a night of joy
> The moon lights up the scar in my heart
> A life forever bright with a longing that never dies
>
> "I Return," To Thuy Yen

BARBARA TRAN

Three Poems

SPIDER: LIFE AFTER 1975

after Galway Kinnell

1

Plumped
with portions
of mosquitoes and flies, eaters
of our blood and shit,
the spider grabs its prey
with its tarsi. With its fangs,
tears into it, ingests our refuse
into its third body. Round

with its kill, safe
in its carapace, the spider clings
to its gauzy web
slung in the corner.

2

She resembles me
in these seven ways:

- she settles where the wind blows her
- she retreats to the corner when troubled
- she doesn't see well
- she uses her legs to get places
- she curls into a ball when she's had enough
- she's a relative of the tick, scorpion, and mite
- she ingests her old home before inhabiting the new

3

Denizen
of the dark, the basement,
where we hide
all we treasure,
the things for which
we have no use
but need
beyond reason
boxes of scrawled letters
meant for loved ones
but never sent, the saliva
of our longing sealed
inside them, lover
of all the places
we have trouble touching,
corners and crannies
we reach for, places
we're unable
to sweep clean
of life's residue, the dirt
and dust and discarded hair
that mark
the hard march
from day
to day, the things
we have let
fall,

she would cover over
all our weak attempts
at living, bind up
our pathetic attachments
to the tangible, our fear
of the unspoken,
spin a web from her gut
to wrap us up
and keep us
from the objects
of our longing

if that
would stop
our manic collection
and hiding

of sentimentalities under the bed.
The common
star is of no interest.
She treasures instead
the domestic, the corner
we call our own, the ceiling
above our beds, to which we cry out
in the dark, the one we beg

for mercy, for aid, for abeyance.

4

In one motion,
a nanny, with the bottom
of her boot,
snatched a spider
and its web
from the corner
where they hung, smashed
them there, once,
twice in the pause
before the third
crushing blow,
the spider's fluids
smacked free
from the bottom
of the boot, and the spider
fell to the ground, scrabbled
under the boards
behind the toilet, left
a glistening outline
of its own carcass
on the wall
that was its home.

5

In the moonlit corner, I sway,
drop the gauzy shirt
from my shoulders, slip
out of my skirt,
and pull

him into me, my legs
clinging, my mouth
searching—a clawed, hungry, half-blind
widow
clasping the man
under me.

6

In the village
I called my own,
I have cowered, been plucked
from my home, pitched
into the unknown.
I have been chased
by men I thought
my brothers, abandoned
by my father. I have scrabbled
for cover, fled
in horror. And on the open sea,
come upon myself
leading
a shimmering, salty wake.

7

And tonight
I find it is late
spring 1975
again: my stomach
bloated, my body
in a ball,
the flies
beginning
to swarm.

RELEASED

He steals
with the ingenuity and hunger

of an average
man. He arrived

in this country
on a paper boat.

He could taste
risk

on his tongue
like a sweet, stolen

kiss. Up at Raybrook,
he hopes

his sister will visit, bring gifts
of the sort

he never gave. The clang
of the cell doors

sometimes sounds
like a tin cup, sometimes

like water, closing
over his head,

sealing his ears, sometimes
a bedroom door

from the wrong side. Occasionally,
the sound

tastes of metal. On her birthday,
he showed up,

took her to the zoo, his arm
around her shoulders.

They watched the seals
feeding. The red leaves

of longing. Planes
zoom overhead, it seems,

hourly. *Give Danny
twenty bucks. He's a good*

*kid, just a little
troubled.* Relentless,

the bedsprings squeak. *Qué
hora es?* The greedy jane

could not be satisfied. What he did
was illegal

because he always
got caught. He would move

to the country, where only the trees
could corrupt him. The hair

on his face feels
rough as the rope they use

for the boats. Risk
leaves a sour taste, like milk,

an hour too late,
thick, on his tongue.

Because children
are cruel, he had to

abandon his sister.
He could still see their mother,

crossing herself,
over and over,

before she touched their dinner
stolen from a dumpster.

It's clear as mud:
paper covers rock.

THE INTERPRETER, POST-'75

after Donald Justice

No longer does the tongue know
the happiness of translation.

It hangs,
a deflated balloon,

sometimes struggling up
against the accusatory finger

of silence. Once
there were missives

to dictate to the hands. Now
there is only rice

to move to the sides, mash
to move to the back.

It wants to brush off
the stale, sugary coat

of rote conversation,
cleanse itself

of the sour residue
of a single language. It dreams

of returning
to the sharp, tart taste

of translation
under fire.

All its efforts produce
uncontrollable drool.

Think of the tongue
swimming.

Think of the tongue
drowning

in its own pool.

ventriloquist _____

what is there in this pungent darkness?
                                        notes drying on shelves
                    hollow mandolin
                                pinch of salt like stars

              there is no wine

                              ( )

this thing which wants to be more than that of mind

a signpost   a directory   a map   of human speech

                    let's rewind the clock
                                        whose hands flow into bodies

          where are you in this pythonine dream?
                                    the air is denser than you

                    walk & it sustains me
              i have no doubts the air also sustains me
                                    these voices deliquescent   unsustained glimmers

( )

the morning light is utterly different

( )

to enter dislocated sleep
                              loiter for the strain

     hung by the voice
                 till the throat dries

( )

     empty & quiet
                does the land speak
 when one walks on it
                        when rain
                              blood drips from branches?

           toward a sky of broken plows

                     there is the work to be done

Three Poems

CAT IN THE WINDOW

Often, late at night, when life feels heavy
I think of poetry, light, almost weightless
When I cannot sleep, I lie down in silence
And think of other people, other days

Suddenly a cat appears in the window
Green eyes staring out like green stars
He sits in the window, silent as a statue
Carved against the shining starry sky

Once again, I love this life without limit
No longer worried and sad, I'm light and free
Through the window, the cat looks out at the sky
Looks out, like the clearest, gentlest poem

CRICKET SONG

Please let me go through life as a cricket
Singing a tiny song in the tender grass
Opening my eyes to shining dewdrops
My words ringing like little bells

Sunbeams gather bell-sounds in the grass
I gather myself in my nest, waiting for night
Sincere, I sing my timeless song
Burrowing in my peaceful green carpet

Don't capture me, don't capture me, my friend
I don't want to be heroic, I don't want glory
People have forced me to charge ahead
In many mortal battles with countrymen

But I just want to bow my head
Although I've won, I'm wounded inside
My friend there, broken foot, burned body—
My friend's wounds, my own wounds ooze
Ignorant people cheered me on

So please just let me be a cricket
Singing transparent words in the silent grass
Looking at silver stars as my song echoes through the field
Drinking in the sweet sun like honey

Please just let me be a cricket
Lying down in the green cradle where I began
While the dying day releases a single dewdrop
That trickles into my soul as a kiss, a tear

WOMAN WEARING BLACK

A woman walks down the road
Spring wind drapes her shoulders
She utters one small phrase
Just so she may hear herself
Just so the wind may hear

There is nothing to regret, she thinks
Flowers and grass grow free, under her feet
There is nothing difficult, she thinks
Step by light step she glides past

Why doesn't she wear purple or pink?
She wears nothing but black
Black clothes like a coffin
Shrouding all her scattered mistakes

She cannot bury the flickering images
The ones she intended to bury
Perhaps her aching heart is the earth
Where that heavy coffin is laid

Oh woman, life is not like that
Why do you foolishly bury yourself?
If you look up at the distant sky you will see
Spring trembling all over, anxiously trembling

Translations by Martha Collins and Thuy Dinh

Esbjerg, on the Coast _____

Luckily the afternoon has turned less cold and at times the sun, through drizzle, lights up the streets and the walls; because at this hour they must be walking in Puerto Nuevo, near the ships or marking time from one dock to another, from the kiosk to the sandwich stand. Kirsten, corpulent, in low heels, a hat crushed down over her yellow hair; and he, Montes, short, bored and nervous, stealing glances at the woman's face, learning without knowing it the names of ships, following, distracted, the maneuvers with the ropes.

I imagine him biting at his mustache while he weighs his desire to shove the woman's peasant body, fattened on the city and leisure, and make it fall into that strip of water between the wet stone and the black iron of the ship, where there is a boiling sound and the space one might keep afloat in narrows. I know they are there because Kirsten came today at noon to look for Montes at the office and I saw them leave, walking toward Retiro, and because she came with her rain-filled face, that face of a statue in winter, face of someone who went on sleeping and did not close her eyes under the rain. Kirsten is heavy, freckled, hardened. Perhaps she still smells of the bodega, of fishermen's nets; perhaps she will come now to have that motionless odor of stables and cream which I imagine she must have in her country.

But at other times they have to go to the wharf at midnight or at dawn, and I think that when the whistles of the ships allow Montes to hear how she advances on the stones, dragging her man's shoes, the poor devil must feel he is plunging into the night on the arm of disgrace. Here in the newspaper is the announcement of the ship departures for this month, and I would swear I can see Montes enduring that immobility from the instant the ship blows its whistle and begins to move off until it is so small that it is not worth the trouble to go on watching; moving at times his eyes—to ask and ask, never understanding, never receiving their answer—toward the fleshy face of the woman, who must be calming down, huddled for long minutes at a time, sad and cold as if it were raining in her dream and she had forgotten to close her very big, almost pretty eyes, tinted the color of the river on days when the mud is not stirred up.

I knew the story, without understanding it well, the very morning Montes came to tell me he had tried to steal from me, had concealed many Saturday and Sunday bets so he could bank them, and now couldn't pay what they had won from him. It didn't matter to me to know why he had done it, but he was furious with the necessity to tell it, and I had to listen while I was thinking of luck, such a friend to his friends, and to them only, and especially so as not to get angry, for in the final analysis if that imbecile had not tried to steal from me, the three thousand *pesos* would have had to come from my pocket. I insulted him till I ran out of words. I used every means I could think of to humiliate him until there remained no doubt that he was a sorry man, a filthy friend, a bastard and a thief; and there was not the shadow of a doubt that he agreed with me, that he had no objection to admitting it to anyone if at any time I had the notion to demand it of him. And also from that Monday it was established that each time I suggested he was contemptible, indirectly, dropping the allusion in whatever chat, no matter what the circumstance, he would have to understand on the spot the meaning of my words and make me aware with a feeling smile, the barest sideward motion of his mustache, that he had understood me and that I was right. We made no agreement in words, but that's the way it has happened ever since. I paid the three thousand *pesos* without a word to him, and weeks I kept him ignorant of whether I would decide to help him or harass him; then I called him in and said yes, I did accept the proposition and he could begin to work in my office for two hundred *pesos* a month, which he would not draw. And in little more than a year, less than a year and a half, he would have paid what he owed and would be free to go off and look for a rope to hang himself with. Of course, he doesn't work for me; I couldn't use Montes for anything since it was impossible for him to go on taking care of the racing bets. I keep this auction and commissions office to be able to relax in, have visitors, and use the telephones. So that he began to work for Serrano, who is my partner in some things and who has the office next to mine. Serrano pays him his salary or pays it to me and keeps him busy all day between Customs and the warehouses, from one end of the city to the other. It doesn't suit me for anyone to know that an employee of mine was not as safe as a betting window at the hippodrome, so nobody does know it.

I believe he told me the story, or almost all of it, the first day, Monday, when he came to see me, cowed as a dog, with his greenish face and a sheen of repulsive congealed sweat on his forehead and the sides of his nose. He must have told me the rest of the things after, in the few times we talked.

It began when winter began, with that first dry cold which makes us all think, without realizing what we are thinking, that the cool and clear air is an air for good business, for escapades with friends, for energetic projects —a luxurious air, perhaps it's that. He, Montes, returned to his house one such day at dark, and he found the woman sitting beside the iron stove staring into the fire burning inside. I don't see the importance of this, but he told it this way and kept repeating it. She was sad and didn't want to say why, and remained sad, with no desire to talk that night and for a week after. Kirsten is fat, sluggish, and must have a very beautiful skin. She was sad and didn't want to tell him what was wrong with her. "Nothing's wrong with me," she said, as all women in all countries say. Afterward she spent her time filling the house with photographs of Denmark, of the king, ministers, landscapes with cows and mountains or whatever they are. She kept saying that nothing was wrong, and that imbecile Montes imagined one thing and another without hitting on anything. Then letters from Denmark began to arrive. He didn't understand a word and she explained that she had written to some distant relatives and now the answers were arriving, although the news was not very good. He said, jesting, that she wanted to go away, and Kirsten denied it. And that night or another not long after, she touched his shoulder when he was about to fall asleep and kept insisting she did not want to go away; he began to smoke and let her have her way in everything while she talked as if she were saying words from memory, from Denmark, the flag with a cross, and a road in the mountain along which she went to church—everything, and with that way of hers, to convince him she was entirely happy with America and with him, until Montes fell peacefully asleep.

For a while letters kept coming and going, and suddenly one night she put out the light when they were in bed and said, "If you let me, I'll tell you something, but you have to listen without saying anything." He said yes and remained stretched out, motionless beside her, letting cigarette ashes fall into the fold of the sheet, his attention fixed like a finger on a trigger, expecting a man to appear in what the woman was telling him. But she spoke of no man, and with a voice harsh and low, as if she had just been crying, told him they could leave bicycles in the street or stores unlocked when going to church or anywhere else, because in Denmark there were no thieves; she told him the trees were bigger and older than trees anywhere in the world and they had a smell, each tree a smell, which could not be mistaken, which kept its uniqueness even when mixed with the other smells of the forest; she said that at dawn one woke up when the sea birds began to scream and the noise of the hunters' guns was heard, and there spring is growing hidden under the snow until it bursts forth suddenly and invades it all like an inundation and people make talk about the thaw. That's the time, in Denmark, when there is most life in the fishing villages.

Also she repeated, *"Esbjerg er naerved kysten,"* and that was what most impressed Montes, although he didn't understand the words: he says it infected him with the desire to cry which filled his woman's voice while she was telling him all that, softly, with that music which without wanting to people use when they are praying. Every now and then. What he did not understand softened him, filled him with compassion for the woman—

heavier than he, stronger—and he wanted to protect her like a lost child. It must be, I think, because the sentence he could not understand was the most distant, the most foreign, what came from the unknown part of her. Since that night he began to feel a compassion which grew and grew, as if she were sick, each day worse, with no possibility of getting well.

So it was that he came to think he would be able to do a great thing, a thing which would do himself good, which would help him live and serve to console him for years. It occurred to him to get the money to pay for Kirsten's journey to Denmark. He went about inquiring when he still did not really think of doing it, and he found out that even two thousand would be enough. Afterwards, he didn't realize he had in him the need to get two thousand *pesos*. It must have been that way, without his knowing what was happening to him. To get the two thousand *pesos* and tell her about it one Saturday night, after dinner in an expensive restaurant, while they were drinking the last glass of good wine. To tell it and see in her face, a little flushed from the dinner and the wine, that Kirsten did not believe him, that she thought he was lying, for a while, then she gave way, slowly, to enthusiasm and joy, then to tears and her decision not to accept. "I'll get over it soon," she would say and Montes would insist until he convinced her, and convinced her besides that he was not trying to leave her and that he would be here waiting for her as long as he must.

Some nights, when in the dark he was thinking of the two thousand *pesos*, or the way to get them, and of the scene in which they would be sitting at a reserved table at Scopelli's one Saturday, with his face serious, with a little joy in his eyes, he began to tell it to her, he began by asking her what day she wanted to depart; some nights when he was dreaming her dream, waiting to fall asleep, again Kirsten talked to him of Denmark. Actually, it was not Denmark, only a part of the country, a very small bit of earth where she had been born, had learned a language, where she had been dancing for the first time with a man and had seen someone she loved die. It was a place which she had lost as a thing is lost, and without being able to forget it. She told him stories, although almost always she repeated the same ones, and Montes believed he himself was seeing there in his bedroom the roads along which she had walked, the trees, the people, and the animals.

Very heavy, contending for the bed without knowing it, the woman lay facing the ceiling, talking; and he always felt secure knowing how her nose arched over her mouth, how her eyes were half-closed between the fine wrinkles, and how Kirsten's chin barely quivered when she pronounced those words in her broken voice, uttered from the depths of her throat, somewhat tiring to be listening to.

Then Montes thought of bank loans, of moneylenders, and even thought I would give him the money. Some Saturday or a Sunday he found himself thinking of Kirsten's voyage while he was with Jacinto in my office answering telephones and taking bets for Palermo or La Plata. There are light days, of scarcely a thousand *peso*s in bets; but sometimes one comes with heavy betting and the money pours in and even goes beyond the five thousand mark. He had to phone me before each race and tell me the state of the bets; if there was much danger—at times one senses it—I tried to cover myself by passing bets on to Vélez, Martín or the Basque. It occurred to him that he could choose not to warn me—that he could conceal three or four of the heaviest bets; face up to, he alone, a thousand tickets; and gamble, if he had the courage, his woman's trip against a bullet in the head. He could do it if he was moved to; Jacinto had no way of finding out how many tickets they played at each phone call. Montes told me he'd been thinking about it for a month; it seems reasonable, it seems such a type must have doubted and agonized a lot before beginning to break into a nervous sweat between telephone rings. But I'd bet a good bit of money he is lying about that; I'd bet he did it in an unwitting moment, made up his mind abruptly, had an attack of confidence and began to steal from me tranquilly beside that beast of a Jacinto, who suspected nothing, who only commented later, "I always did say that wasn't many tickets for an afternoon like that." I'm sure Montes had a hunch and felt he was going to win and had not planned it.

That's how he began to pocket bets which mounted to three thousand *peso*s, how he began to pace up and down the office, sweating and desperate, glancing at the racing forms, glancing at Jacinto's gorilla body with its raw silk shirt, glancing through the window at the parking lot, which began to fill up with autos at dusk. That's the way it was, when he began to find out he was losing and the dividends were growing, hundreds of *peso*s at each drop of the phone, how he came to be sweating that special sweat of cowards, greasy, greenish, congealed, which his face bore when at Monday noon, finally, he had in his legs strength enough to return to the office and talk to me.

He had told her before trying to steal from me; he had told her that something very important and very good was going to happen, that he had a gift for her which was incomparable and was not a concrete thing she could touch. So that afterwards he felt obliged to speak to her and tell her of his disgrace; and it was not at a reserved table at Scopelli's nor drinking an imported Chianti, but in the kitchen of their house, sucking at the *mate bombilla* while her round face, in profile and red from the reflection, watched the fire leap inside the iron stove. I don't know how much they must have cried. After that he arranged to pay me by working it off; and she got a job.

The other part of the story began when she, a while after, got in the habit of being away from their house at hours which had nothing to do with her work. She arrived late when they were to meet, and at times she got up very late at night, dressed, and went out without a word. He was not moved to say anything, was not moved to say much and confront her face to face, because they are living on what she earns, and from his work with Serrano comes nothing more than a drink which I pay for now and then. So that he kept his mouth shut and accepted his turn to bother her with his bad humor, a different bad humor, but added to that which had come over them ever since the afternoon Montes tried to steal from me and which I think will not leave them till the day they die. He was suspicious and kept feeding himself on stupid ideas until one day he followed her and saw her go to the port and drag her shoes over the stones, alone, and stand there a long time, looking toward the water, near but apart from the people who go to say goodbye to the travelers. As in the stories she had told him, there was no man. This time they talked, and she explained it to him. Montes also insists on something else which has no importance: he argues, as if I couldn't believe it, that she explained it in her normal voice and that she was not sad or hateful or ashamed. She told him she always went to the port, at any hour, to watch the ships which depart for Europe. He was afraid for her and wanted to struggle against this, he wanted to convince her that what she was doing was worse than staying at home; but Kirsten went on talking in her normal voice and said it did her good to do it and she would keep going to the port to see how the ships leave, to wave some farewell or simply gaze until her eyes grew tired, as often as she could.

And he ended by convincing himself that it is his duty to accompany her, that in this way he pays in installments the debt he owes her as he is paying the one he owes me; and now, on this Saturday afternoon, as on so many nights and noons, in good weather or sometimes in a rain over the other rain which is always watering her face, they go off together, beyond Retiro, walk along the wharf until the ship leaves, mix a little with the people with overcoats, suitcases, flowers and handkerchiefs, and when the ship begins to move, after the whistle blows, they stand rigid and stare, stare until they can no longer, each one thinking of very different and hidden things, but agreeing without knowing it on hopelessness and on the feeling that each one is alone, which is always startling when we begin to think about it.

Translation by H. E. Francis

Hilario, El Carretero del Barrio

Arroyo Naranjo, Cuba, Circa 1969

He rang a bell he rigged by the wooden slat of his cart, where the cracks came together with wire and rusty nails. Twice he rang it, then his voice boomed down the street: *"Maní tostado, maní. Se afilan cuchillos, tijeras, achas."* He sold roasted peanuts. He also sharpened scissors, knives, axes. *"Pan dulce, pan dulce y caliente."* Sweet, hot bread.

The boys in the neighborhood snuck up and rode on the back of his cart as he wound up and down the street, around the corner. Hilario knew we were back there, dangling our legs from the back, giggling. It was fine with him as long as we didn't steal a *cucurucho de maní,* his peanuts, or a piece of his bread. The bread looked like the arms of angels under the pieces of wax paper held down with clothespins and rocks so that the wind wouldn't blow them off or flies get on the bread.

When our parents gave us money, we bought the bread, such sticky, sweet, caramel-scented bread, which we ate with great gusto in the shade of the plantain trees by the sidewalk. When Hilario sharpened knives and scissors, orange sparks kicked up over his arms and his face. Each time, he'd stop, lick his finger, then run it over the edge to check the sharpness. His fingertips were maps of cut skin, never healing, growing into calluses.

Our fathers said he was the best machete sharpener anywhere, leaving a shiny sliver of sharp on the edge of the blade.

Our parents felt sorry for Hilario and his cart, the way he had to make a living, so they gave us money to buy things from him. He was a skinny man with very dark, burnt-sugar skin. His deep-set eyes never looked at you straight. Drunk, or else there was something wrong with the way he looked up to people, was the story we always heard.

Then there was the missing leg, which, no matter how bad we treated him, we never dared bring up. We learned early never to mention the leg because it could cost us a couple of teeth. Or, we were afraid Hilario would, in one swift swoop, cut off one of our ears with the sharpened dagger he kept tucked between his rope belt and his tattered pants.

On his arms were faded, green-inked numbers that everyone knew were from the years he'd spent at La Cabana, Cuba's worst prison for political prisoners. Our parents said Hilario had spent twenty years there, starting with the Machado regime, then Bautista's, and then Fidel's.

Everything that could be wrong with a person was wrong with him. He stuttered and gasped as he tried to speak. Because he was missing his right leg, whenever he climbed down from the cart to sharpen the knives, scissors, or axes we brought him, his pant leg came loose and dangled there like the trunk of an elephant. Two of his fingers were missing, the stumps wiggling as he moved his hands. He chain-smoked, so his fingers were dirty yellow, with half moons of grime and grease under his long nails.

When we made fun of him, calling him *El cojo,* he told us to go fuck our mothers. We loved to hear him say this, so we called him names all the time. And when we got him riled up, he'd start coughing and have to stop to catch his breath. *"Cabrones!"* he'd shout back at us. *"Algun día se van acordar de mi!"* Once he told us the story of how he'd been a fighting-cock trainer in Las Villas, where his father gambled at the fights. He said he loved the way a rooster's feather caught the light, held its iridescence for one brief moment in a flash of silver and gold.

He dreamt of one day owning the best fighting cocks in the land, said he knew how to train them. His voice shook with conviction, and so we believed him for as long as we got to ride on his cart. The cart was pulled by an old, mangy mule that kept shitting all over the place, including its own hind legs. Nobody knew Hilario's whole story—not us, not our parents—and he never told us anything about himself, other than the stories of the cock fights.

When we angered him, when he thought we didn't care about his roosters, he'd scream that we were all sissies, unable to tell the difference between a rooster and a fighting cock. *"Un gallo campeón,"* he would say, then call us *gallinas.* Nothing but a bunch of hens. If we caught up to him on the road home from school, we would ask him for a ride, and he'd give us one as long as we later went inside our houses and brought out money to buy his peanuts and bread. His cart creaked and rocked and got us there.

For years Hilario plied our neighborhood, and we came to depend on his stops, on his raspy voice calling out, *"Pan dulce caliente! Maní tostado!"*

Once, we even saw the stump of his missing leg. Right at the knee where the doughy flesh folded and knotted into itself. The day we saw it, he was wearing cut-off pants. His good leg was skinny and covered with scars, as though someone had taken a machete and tried to hack him down. Sometimes we brought him cigarette butts and half-smoked cigars we found on the street, and he'd trade peanuts for them so that he could shred the tobacco and roll himself new smokes.

Nobody really knew where he lived, though some said he came to Arroyo Naranjo from Calabazar, where everyone also knew him. He traveled as far as the airport in Rancho Boyeros, where he loved to stop and watch Russian and Cubana Airlines planes take off and land. He once promised to take us there with him to watch. Then one day he stopped coming through, and for days we missed him, looked for him up and down our streets, around the corners. No cart in sight, no trail of mule dung. Hilario disappeared from our neighborhood.

Our parents didn't know what had happened to him. Rumors set in. He'd been arrested for trafficking in the black market. He'd been accused by the CDR of counterrevolutionary activities. He'd hung himself from the branch of a ceiba tree. He'd gone crazy and been taken to Masorra. He'd left the country clandestinely on a boat. On a raft. None of us knew what to believe, but our days were never the same. Nobody else came through the neighborhood to sell us the sweet bread of our childhoods. Or salted, roasted peanuts.

We walked the dusty streets of our neighborhood, turning to the wind in hopes we'd catch his voice, the *clip-clop* of his mule. Our shadows began to catch up to us, and scare us. These beginning absences in our own lives, reminders of how long we still had to go. Hilario, his mule and cart, his gnarled hands, his foggy, distant eyes, the way his empty pant leg moved in the wind, like the broken and tattered flag of our complete and unequivocal surrender in our childhoods.

Coded Message

1

I believe

That my father
In his dying

Prowled the corridors
Of Saint Joseph's Hospital
Looking for stained glass

Searching particularly
For a sword of white light
Next to a wide curve
Of cobalt blue

Those were Mary's colors
& the colors
Of a palomino
On a high ridge
Against the sky in West Omaha

2

On that thin white sheet

My father never gave up his dying
He gave up the deep tan of his hands

He gave up the images
Of his house on Cass Street
Deep in the skull under his blue eyelids

Some mornings
He seemed
To give up his breath
To the shivers

When a quiet nun entered his room &
Threaded a rosary about his fingers
Until the silver-threaded locust beans
Would slide to a white tile floor   A tiny
Jesus bouncing in the glow on sun-washed wax

3

On that thin white sheet

My father kept trying
To leave his body on Earth

He tried to leave
Through the thick grooves
Of those Irish toenails

He tried to leave
Through hidden wisdom teeth
Then through two front teeth
With their pain-filled silver helmets

At the end   He kept trying
To float up the IV drip   Past
The iced needles of insulin   Into
The calm syllables of coma
Whispering his name in a new language

4

Months later I walked miles in snow

To the hospital & sat
In a chair in that corner

Staring for hours
Toward a bright white wall
Bleached by sunlight

I stared even longer
At the sheet
Tight   Flat   White   Taut
Speechless as a sun-rinsed cloud

I was
Quiet as floor shadow
Silent as a quart of black paint
Still as a bottle of India ink
I have never left that room   Not once

Three Poems

RECESSIONAL

He who traveled the world to find
pure distance found only
the next range always receding.

One destination, many names—
Patagonia, Archangel
where tears freeze before they fall.

Even the next room appeared
remote, the woman in it, humming,
hard to reach as the nearest star.

GOUACHE

Sketch of a heavy man in soft grays
and black seated against the faded backdrop
of an old city, Cracow perhaps.

He's not waiting for color to give him life,
or for the glass of darkness on the table
to redden as the artist might have hoped.

He leans to pluck an improvised guitar.
The woman sitting beside him opens her mouth
as if to sing, as if to sing the silence.

DAUGHTERS OF MUSIC

Daughters of music, brought low these days,
sing on though the wheel is broken, the almond tree
blighted in blighted fields.

We scarcely catch their drift, sisters of wind,
voices of smoke lamenting the broken pitcher
left at the dry well.

Too late now to comfort us, they carol
into the night, lovely, meaningless songs,
obsolete as candles.

Rivers _____

All week, Mr. Toan kept busy changing the oil in his car, fixing the brakes, and adjusting the engine hoses. The gold Toyota, still fairly new, was a gift from Vinh, his eldest son. He had received it after he had been in America for three months.

It was the end of autumn; by the time his three kids came home from their jobs or from school, it was already dark. They didn't say anything about their father's tinkering with the car. Cuong, who had changed his name to Cowen, once told him, in English, that he should just take it to a mechanic. Cuong was the last son, born only three months before the end of the war or, as Mr. Toan would say, when they lost the country. Mrs. Toan escaped to the United States with Cuong, his two older brothers, and his sister. Mr. Toan was captured while stationed in Quang Tri and was taken to the Truong Son mountains as a prisoner.

Mr. Toan's kids always stayed in their rooms. They listened to music, watched TV, or were on the phone for hours. Or they'd be in front of the computer. They'd show their faces at dinner, chomping pizza, hamburgers, or fried chicken. They were such animals. If their mother asked about their days, they'd mumble back their answers. They disappeared into their rooms again after taking turns doing the dishes. Mr. Toan was just a ghost. Didn't say much or smile, and laughed even less. Yesterday, Cuong asked his mother what his father was doing with the car. His mother said, Oh, well, only your dad would know. I don't know. She spoke in English, and Mr. Toan could catch just a word or two. He'd studied English for nine months, from the time he arrived in America. But he was old and tired. Whatever he learned, he forgot. His old friends would ask. He'd smile. Oh, I'll survive. Cut grass for a living. What do I need English for? The more I study, the more I forget. The less I study, the less there is to forget. If I don't study, I don't forget.

After eating, Mr. Toan would go to the basement to wash his clothes. Normally, he'd sit and read the newspapers he found in the Vietnamese grocery store downtown. His wife left him alone.

Over the weekend, Mr. Toan cooked a big pot of noodle soup. Vinh, whose name was now Victor, ate two bowls. Each of the others only had a small bowl, but didn't even finish that. Cuong was glued to the phone, making plans to meet his friends at some restaurant. Loan (Lou-Ann) and Tuan (Tony) were out until late. Mr. Toan stayed home with his wife but said nothing much. Mrs. Toan's maiden name had been Van; now she was Vanna. She was a real estate agent and was doing well but had to put up with demanding hours.

On Saturday morning, Mrs. Toan asked her husband to come along when she was showing some houses. She could drop him off at their friends'. Mr. Toan asked her to stay home because he wanted to talk to her. She said, Whatever it is, it can wait. I have an appointment—I have to go. He went back to tinkering with his car. He had been an officer in the armored-cars division and wasn't afraid of tanks, so the Toyota was no big deal—except for the electronic parts that were too modern for him. Finished with the engine, he went to place a few cardboard boxes in the trunk. In the past weeks, he'd picked up things from both Vietnamese and American stores and put them in the boxes.

Sunday night, everyone went to bed early. No one said anything to him, and no one wanted to hear much from him. The weekend had gone by like any other.

Monday morning, everyone left the house like clockwork. Mrs. Toan left at a quarter to eight. So did Loan and Vinh. One was a medical intern; the other had just graduated as an electrical engineer. Cuong went to school. Each had a car. When Mr. Toan came to America, he was pleased to find the kids had done well in school. He was grateful to his wife.

Mr. Toan drove off at nine. He normally got to the English and vocational school at nine fifteen, and classes would start at nine thirty. The English teacher was his daughter's age, but still, she was a teacher. The guy who taught his electronic-assembly class was a fat American, always breathing as if he was about to have a heart attack in the middle of the lecture.

Today, Mr. Toan didn't go to his classes. He threw a small suitcase in the backseat and took the car on the freeway. In the afternoon, when Mrs. Toan came home, Cuong handed her a letter written in Vietnamese, which he couldn't read. Mr. Toan said he wasn't sure when he'd be back.

After a three-hour drive, Mr. Toan was sleepy. It was late autumn and there was a bit of sunshine. Mr. Toan rolled down the window to let some cold air in, but still felt tired. He pulled into a restaurant, the kind you often see alongside freeways. He parked the car, went inside, and ordered a cup of coffee and some food. When the waiter brought him a plate of grilled beef, he reached into his bag for a vial of fish sauce and a plastic bag containing some hot peppers. He ate his meal with an air of satisfaction. Then he asked for some hot water, making himself a cup of what is called in the highlands of Viet Nam "sweet-grass tea." It was a gift from some of his former soldiers.

Mr. Toan drove for the rest of the day, spending that night at a cheap motel, the kind you find by the side of the freeway. America was full of freeways; it was a huge country. There were places with massive meadows and tens of thousands of cows. How he wished Viet Nam could have just a bit of this wealth; the people would be better off. But Viet Nam suffered a kind of sick fate that lingered, from one generation to the next, from one century to another, from one king to the next. Could any amount of wealth change such a fate?

Mr. Toan left the hotel early in the morning. Every few hours, he'd stop to have a light meal, each accompanied by a bit of fish sauce and hot peppers. Each ended with a cup of the sweet-grass tea. Then he'd be off again. For the first day, he was able to contemplate the scenery on either side of the freeway. On the second day and thereafter, he kept his eyes open but could only see the films projecting inside his mind. A couple of times, he sang a few lines from the epic poem "Tale of Kieu." A couple of other times, he shook his head, smiling to himself.

On the third day, he arrived in a big city. The hills and meadows and trees had disappeared. In front of him and to either side of the freeway were skyscrapers. Near the horizon, a river. Mr. Toan decided to rest.

He checked into a hotel. The room rate took him aback for a moment, but he said nothing. He left his suitcase in the car, bringing inside just a shirt and a pair of trousers that he would put on after he'd showered. Looking in the phone book, he found a Vietnamese restaurant. He dialed the number, asked for directions, and hung up after thanking the person on the line.

The restaurant was on the riverbank. Mr. Toan parked on the hill, looking down at the river. He thought of others. The Han River in Da Nang. The little Thu Bon River in Hoi An. The Bach Dang River in Saigon, and the River of Perfume in Hue. He even remembered the Red River, which he had last seen as a boy, just before the country was separated in half.

He shivered. Autumn was fading away, winter approaching. The currents in the river were running swiftly. This kind of river could not give rise to poems or folk songs full of romance. There could be no songs about a sampan gliding across to the other side, taking a lover away from his love. He wondered whether America had a river that carried the meaning of separation, the way the Ben Hai River did for him and his people.

In twenty years in the military, he had traveled to all parts of his country. He had led his tanks to countless rivers and embankments; he'd ordered his troops and his guns to tear apart the land that was his. Now he had been dragged into the swift currents of a life in exile.

America was a funny place, full of weird customs that had taken root in his wife and children. Mr. Toan thought he'd better get to know America. Only a trip like this could help him. Then he could return to a cheerful life with his wife and the kids. It wasn't their fault that he hadn't been around when they had had to leave the country. It certainly wasn't their fault that they'd changed after all the years in America. Everybody changes, everything changes. He needed to change, too.

And yet, in all the days driving across America, he wasn't sure his loneliness was going away. He still felt the alienation. And in this city by the river, he had come to this restaurant for the smell of lemongrass or fresh cilantro.

The place wasn't too crowded. Mr. Toan was seated at a corner table. He borrowed a newspaper and asked for a bowl of noodles with rare beef and uncooked bean sprouts. He read and ate slowly, and he didn't see the old man come in.

The man was perhaps seventy-five or eighty years old, his hair thin and gone completely white. The hair was still brushed tightly back, like before, but had lost its black sheen. The face had grown gaunt.

The man surveyed the restaurant for a second, then recognized Mr. Toan. Hey, Toan, the man said. Where'd you come from?

Mr. Toan raised his head, opening his mouth. But he couldn't say anything.

When the man approached, Mr. Toan stood up. He was able to let out two words: Mr. President.

The man grabbed Mr. Toan's shoulders. You came here, too, huh? When did you get here?

Not too long ago, Mr. President.

The man waved a hand, dismissing Mr. Toan. Don't talk like that. Nguyen Van Thieu's no longer a president. Just a refugee, like all of you. Sit. Sit down.

Both men sat down. Mr. Thieu turned to the waiter behind the counter. Bring another bowl of *pho*. Turning back to Mr. Toan, Mr. Thieu asked about his health and resettling in America, and shook his head listening to stories about people in Viet Nam being rounded up and sent to reeducation camps. They mentioned names of men who had been in the army with them a long time ago. When the restaurant owner brought out the bowl of *pho*, the two were talking about current events and the situation in Viet Nam. Mr. Thieu talked a great deal. Mr. Toan merely answered his questions.

When they had drunk their last bit of tea, Mr. Thieu looked tired. He was no longer criticizing the men in power in Viet Nam. He lowered his voice. What a shame; if you'd been in Ban Me Thuot then—. Without news, I suspected you'd been caught in Quang Tri. Now everybody says I gave bad orders. Mr. Thieu waved his hand. What else could I have done? No one was able to take charge. Everything had to wait until I gave the orders.

Mr. Toan kept his head down, looking into his cup of tea as though it contained some kind of light that could illuminate the past. After a while, he said, Let me ask you. Looking back, how do you want history to record your role?

Forget it, Mr. Thieu said. Why talk about such a thing? I did all I could. Losing the country was the fate of us all, of all the people. And if I say this, don't think I'm crazy. If things weren't the way they turned out in April 1975, how could there be a million, two million Vietnamese here in America? . . . Now I've got to go.

They settled the bill and walked out together.

Mr. Toan mumbled, A million and a half Vietnamese in America.

Mr. Thieu gave a chuckle. That's right: a million and a half. You've got to work so hard here. I wonder whether any one of us could still do anything for the old country. But you have to be proud. Our people are excellent. Everybody is doing so well. The kids are doing well.

Mr. Toan seemed a bit lost. There are still so many back home, miserable. But he swallowed this thought, saying nothing to Mr. Thieu. He followed Mr. Thieu out to the gray Jaguar parked behind his Toyota.

Mr. Thieu got inside and closed the door. He rolled down the window. I'm happy for you. Keep trying. Make sure your kids finish school, and take care of them. But don't let them waste their talents on this country. We came here so that we could one day help our country; we didn't come here to help America get rich, did we?

Mr. Toan smiled, said goodbye, and got into his car just as Mr. Thieu put his car in gear. The Jaguar lurched forward, rear-ending the Toyota.

Mr. Toan had just released the hand brake. The Toyota went down the hill.

The thought that went through Mr. Toan's mind at that moment was centered on the words of the old president. *Make sure your kids finish school, and take care of them. But don't let them waste their talents on this country.*

That was Mr. Toan's last thought before his car plunged into the river, into the torrent of water.

At that moment, it was winter in America. The river currents were forceful, rushing forward like time.

That whole winter, Mrs. Toan—Van, or Vanna—and the kids waited for news from Mr. Toan. They sought news from friends, the vocational school, and veterans organizations throughout America. They went in and out of police stations and talked for hours to hospital information officers. They even went into a morgue when they learned about an Asian man who had died without being identified.

There were times when Mrs. Toan thought he had taken up with some woman, or had taken a new wife, perhaps someone he had had a relationship with in Viet Nam during the years she had been killing herself to raise the children in America. Then she thought, I have to keep hope alive. He'll come back soon. In America, there were all kinds of people with mental problems, doing things no one could understand. And Mr. Toan had been a combat soldier, then imprisoned for many years. Sometimes, watching TV, Mrs. Toan would learn about a shooting incident at a restaurant or a post office, and she would be terrified. Sometimes, when the phone rang late in the night, she would feel a sharpness in her heart.

Mrs. Toan and the children went back and forth between a state of despair and one of heightened anxiety. Winter faded; spring came with brighter lights and cherry blossoms along the streets near their house. Summer came and went. But there was simply no news from her husband.

The old president had also gone through a gloomy winter.

He had been shocked to see the car rolling down the hill and into the river. He'd jumped out of his car and rushed to the embankment. The currents rolled on, and the Toyota sank within seconds. Disappeared.

Mr. Thieu had panicked for a few seconds. Should he call the police? Should he stay around? It felt like the old days. Quang Tri. Ban Me Thuot. Responsibilities. Nha Trang. An Loc. Responsibilities. History.

This time, however, no one had abandoned him. He had just put the car in gear too quickly. How could there be so many accidents in a lifetime? And tragedies? And how could the fate—the lives—of so many rest in his two hands?

In the end, Mr. Thieu had returned to his car and left the hill.

He never ate at that restaurant again. And he stopped visiting with his old friends, his old soldiers. Sometimes, he would answer his phone and utter a few words to his former soldiers, but he stayed away, absolutely, from giving any further advice.

History would later mark this as the beginning of his final period of silence.

Mr. Toan sat helplessly inside the Toyota. Outside was the roiling mass of water.

The Toyota bobbed about in the water. Mr. Toan had a thought: I was once an armored-infantry man. Now I am going to die at the bottom of a river, like a sailor.

The Toyota kept rolling around. Mr. Toan closed his eyes. This is what it would be like to be inside the belly of a dragon, he thought. Then another thought came to him: I am a former officer of the Army of the Republic of South Viet Nam. I came to America as part of a reunification program. A flight out of Viet Nam, into Bangkok, Thailand, then on to the United States. I didn't have to suffer like others. Take the boat people, for example. And here I am, rolling around in water and drowning. Oh well, we all die, one way or another. It's too bad this is Vinh's car. Otherwise, dying is just dying, even if you die in a torrent of water.

That was when Mr. Toan heard the shouts.

The deluge! The deluge, do you hear me?! There's nothing else—just the deluge!

The shouts became louder and louder. Mr. Toan opened his eyes, trying to see out the windshield, still covered with muddy water. In front of the car, he saw the shadow of a short man with a square body. And then he could see the man wore a white suit, looking quite dignified.

The man appeared clearer. Mr. Toan then acted out of instinct. He stepped on the brake pedal, switched gears, and pulled the hand brake. Then he opened the door and got out of the car. The Toyota was sitting on a nice green lawn; it sure wasn't in a river.

Mr. Toan looked down at his feet, taking tentative steps on the grass. Then he raised his head, opening his mouth. But he couldn't say anything.

The man in the white suit stood by a porch. But this was no ordinary house. Mr. Toan was shocked to find the Gia Long presidential palace in the middle of a humid day in Saigon. The drops of water on the Toyota were glinting under the sun.

The man in the white suit kept one hand behind his back and pointed the other to the sky, index finger straight up. His eyes were full of fury.

He shouted again. Did you hear me?!

Mr. Toan was able to let out three words: Yes, Mr. President.

The man turned to take three steps to the left, then turned around, three steps to his right. Then he shouted. Ngo Dinh Diem never says anything wrong! Do you hear me?!

Mr. Toan stood at attention to face the man's rage.

Let me tell you: Behind me is the deluge!

Mr. Diem stressed each of his words now. The deluge!

Après moi, le déluge! The deluge! The deluge. Once Ngo Dinh Diem is gone, you all will become a deluge, destroying everything. Wash away all the things I've built all my life. You are devils.

Mr. Toan stood very still.

Mr. Diem pointed a finger at Mr. Toan. Go and tell your people: Ngo Dinh Diem never says anything wrong! Behind me is the deluge. People who would damage this nation, destroy the people of this country!

The president of the first republic waved his arm. Now go away! Bring your troops, deploy them carefully, and surround the palace with your tanks. And if you don't have an order from me, don't make a move!

Mr. Toan had no control of his mind. It was as if he had left his body and could see himself from afar. He could see himself raising an arm in a military salute to the president, stomping his right foot, and then stepping back two paces before turning around.

It was hot in Saigon, and the sun was bright. It made Mr. Toan's shadow long and dark on the lawn.

Mr. Toan saw himself wave an arm to signal invisible soldiers somewhere nearby. Then he saw himself driving the Toyota off the palace grounds. The car rolled for a short distance on the big boulevard before drifting to a stop by the sidewalk.

Mr. Toan left the car and opened the rear door. He pulled out a canvas army seat, sat down, and reached for the pair of binoculars hanging from his chest. He placed the binoculars to his eyes and surveyed the surroundings. The boulevard ran straight from where he sat to where he could no longer see. He could make out the red-brick church at one end.

In the park he could see the big trees. The lower half of their trunks was painted white, and in the shade of each were silhouettes of men with shaved heads, sitting motionless in the lotus position, one hand raised to the chest.

After a while, Mr. Toan put down the binoculars, leaned back on the car, and fell asleep.

The summer moment carried no wind. Not a breeze. It was boiling hot. Silence had settled in. Even the cicadas didn't bother: it was too hot to sing.

About half an hour later, Mr. Toan felt a finger scraping his shoulder. He opened his eyes and looked to his left. A stooped man flashed him a smile, which seemed to come more from his eyes. The old man was playing with the tuft of white hair on his chin.

The man said, Good afternoon, Mr. Officer.

Mr. Toan stared at the man, vaguely recognizing him, but couldn't for the life of him say exactly who it was. Mr. Toan said nothing.

The old man said, It's hot, and placed his palm on his baldpate, wiping it clean of his sweat. Mr. Officer, dear, let's see, how about this? I'm pretty old, so why don't we just talk to each other as if you're my nephew and I'm your uncle. Let's be like family, shall we? I'm telling you the truth now. I've been watching you sleep for nearly two months. But you slept so soundly, and your uncle here is anxious, but I didn't have the heart to wake you up. I know you must be so tired, in this heat, and to tell the truth, what young man wouldn't be in these times. Isn't your uncle right? Now, give me one of your perfumed cigarettes.

The old man pointed at Mr. Toan's shirt pocket. Mr. Toan reached for it, noticed something bulging, and saw that it was indeed a pack of Red Ruby cigarettes, the kind they sell at military exchange posts. Mr. Toan remembered that it had been years since he gave up smoking—since he was captured and taken to the prison camps up in the Truong Son mountains. How could he have cigarettes? He gave one to the old man and slipped the pack into his pocket.

I'm not lying to you, the old man went on without thanking him. I do need to ask something else of you. The man lit the cigarette with his bony hands. He let out a puff of smoke. It's true I'm in a bit of trouble. Enemies among our own people. White devils, too. Everybody's chasing me around. It's so hard.

The old man sucked on the cigarette again. This is a nice smell. In the old days, I could smoke this perfumed tobacco. That was when I lived in France. Hey, your uncle here knows: you're about to bring your car and your troops to the central province. Don't be upset. They report everything to me. Rest assured: nothing will happen to you.

Mr. Toan looked around, unable to see any of his soldiers.

Oh, they've all run away. Your staff officer went to the other side. Took his unit down to Thu Duc. I know, I know. But it doesn't matter. Uncle and nephew should get going, get the show on the road, as they say in America.

Mr. Toan looked at the old man.

Why are you looking at Uncle so? If I don't come with you, who will show you the way? And if Uncle should set out on his own, I'd risk being captured and sent to prison. Oh, how I hate prison. I am terrified of prison. Terrified. *C'etait simplement effroyable.* But right now, I'm in disguise, an infiltrator, *hah!* Now—if I don't go with you, then I've lost my usual shrewdness, haven't I? I love it. Me, an infiltrator, traveling with a colonel in the puppet army!

The old man's hand went back to his white beard. Let me tell you, my nephew, that if you don't leave right now, you might end up in prison yourself. It's hard to tell these days. Who can you trust? Whose side are you on? Can you really tell? Let's just go. You and me, uncle and nephew together as one. I'll reward you later. For your glorious, selfless contribution.

Mr. Toan had no control of his mind. All these people. Teaching him, admonishing him, shouting at him, asking for favors. And he did everything that was asked, followed orders. He saw his body rise, open the car door, and crawl inside. The old man quickly walked around to the other side and jumped in the passenger's seat.

The Toyota slowly rolled away from the sidewalk just as there was a roar in the sky. A jet fighter was diving down, tearing through the space above the two men.

The jet sent a missile straight into the presidential palace. It exploded on impact, and the second floor burst into flames.

Mr. Toan looked around, catching sight of the men who had been sitting under the trees. Monks. They were running in all directions, their saffron robes billowing like butterfly wings.

The old man said something. Mr. Toan could only catch a few words. I told them . . . firmness and determination . . . running . . . undignified . . . a cigarette . . .

The old man put his fingers on Mr. Toan's shoulders. He mechanically reached for the cigarettes, handing the whole pack to the old man. The jet fighter had disappeared. He could hear the old man clearly now. Later, some of them will become important members of the politburo. Give up their saffron robes, *hah!* How do I know everything, huh?

Mr. Toan couldn't understand all that was said because he was having to deal with a mob of people that had suddenly appeared on the street in front of him. People ran in all directions, like the monks. There were bicycles and pedicabs and the small gold-and-blue taxis.

A tank turned the corner and headed straight for the Toyota. Soldiers emerged and blocked Mr. Toan's advance. One of them pointed a gun in Mr. Toan's face. The old man sunk into his seat, pulling his knees up to his forehead.

The soldier shouted out something, then put his gun away. He raised his hand to his beret and saluted Mr. Toan. Turning around, he waved the tank away and motioned the nearby people and soldiers to clear a space for the Toyota. Mr. Toan inched forward, turning toward the road circling the red-brick church.

The soldier walked alongside the Toyota for a few feet, then looked inside again. His smile turned into a frown. He recognized the old man. In a flash, he had his gun pointed to the sky and let out a hail of bullets.

Mr. Toan stepped on the gas. The car shot forward, climbed up on the sidewalk, and scattered people. Mr. Toan kept steering the Toyota through the crowds until he regained control of the car. Then he drove off toward a street he recognized, but it had a new name: Catinat.

Uncle, he asked, are the French back?

No, no. The old man smiled. They're all gone now. They took off soon after Giap dealt them the deadly blow. How else would Brother Dong be able to speak so forcefully in Geneva? Don't you want a cigarette?

Mr. Toan shook his head, concentrating on the road. Crowds of people were crouching by the sides of buildings. Some were crisscrossing the street.

The old man smiled again. But that was some trick the brothers here in the South played on me. If you didn't sign the treaty, how could I insist on elections? It was war all over again. But that was a good trick. I like cunning people. Turn—turn right. Giap was like that. Very smart. Good old Giap. Can't control his family, though.

The Toyota left the downtown streets and headed into the Chuong Duong port. At the sight of the river, Mr. Toan felt a shock.

The old man said, That's where your uncle took off. Do you like water? I love water. I sat on the ship for four years before we landed in New York. I was a cook's assistant, always in the kitchen. But I found excuses once in a while to go up to the deck so I could look down at the vast ocean. It was so lovely. You people in the South have a lot of rivers; you must love water, too. It's not by chance that in our language the words for *water* and *nation* are the same.

Mr. Toan held a tight grip on the steering wheel, avoiding the throngs of people running toward the docked ships. He decided not to listen anymore to the old man.

He turned the Toyota toward the road along the quay and headed out of town. An hour later, he was traveling on Highway 1, heading north, rushing past the rubber plantations.

On the third day, they reached Quang Ngai. They didn't plan to stop. They had not eaten or slept in the three days, but Mr. Toan felt neither tired nor hungry. The highway cut through fields of golden rice stalks; it was peaceful scenery, with columns of smoke rising from the clusters of villages on the horizon. That was when they heard gunshots. It went on for fifteen minutes or so.

Mr. Toan drove toward the sound of the barrage. He stopped the car by the entrance to a village and followed the old man out.

They found hundreds of bodies. Dead old people. Dead babies. There was blood on the ground, so much of it, and the stench was so bad that Mr. Toan threw up.

There were bodies everywhere, piled on top of one another.

The old man shook his head. This must be My Lai. You watch. The Americans will pay a high price for this. It's not such a big deal—all these dead people. Before, when our people went overboard with the land-reform program, many more died. They wouldn't listen to your uncle and allowed our cadres to become savages. But this incident the Americans won't be able to hide. And it will cost them the goodwill of the world. It'll be our PR victory.

Mr. Toan stared at the old man.

He decided he would turn around, go to the car, and drive away without the old man.

Oh well, said the old man. I can make my way from here. I'll follow the trail up in the mountains. Hope I won't get hit by a bomb. Hey, let me give you some money. Let's just say it's for gas. I hope you won't be court-martialed for driving me out here. Let me just give you this money. It's not much, but Party policy prevents me from taking advantage of the people. You don't want it? I'll just place it on the dashboard, all right?

The man placed a stack of bank notes on the dashboard. They looked old and had a picture of Ho Chi Minh in the right-hand corner.

It was now midafternoon. A storm was coming in from the east. The clouds were thick and swift, the rain poured down in an instant, and the wind blew through the car windows and scattered the bills with the image of Ho Chi Minh.

Mr. Toan soon ran into a muddy stretch on the highway. The car slid from side to side, finally slipping down a slope and rolling over. The wheels pointed toward the raging sky.

Mr. Toan hit his head against the steering wheel and passed out.

The sound of the hoes and hammers was getting louder. So were the cries of people, shouting in unison to coordinate their efforts. The car rocked back and forth in the hands of the villagers and soldiers.

Mr. Toan came around and looked about him before realizing that there were people outside and that they were running thick ropes underneath the car. No one seemed to know he was inside. He tried twisting his body a little, and the pain nearly killed him. He could feel his feet, but had no idea what position his body and limbs were in. He kept wiggling despite the

pain. At one point, he looked out of the part of the windshield that had survived the accident. Most of it was covered in mud, but he could see some
objects: large, shapeless, casting dark shadows on the windshield.

Elephants. That's what they were. Huge elephants. It took a moment for
him to realize that the people were using elephants to pull the car out and
turn it over.

The elephants let out eerie sounds that were somewhere between a shout
and an amplified sigh. The car was bouncing under their force.

Mr. Toan was thrown about inside and passed out again.

When he woke up, he realized he was prostrate on a bamboo platform.

A man wearing a colorful robe embroidered with dragons and phoe-
nixes was sitting next to him. He had armored shoulders and metal gloves,
and his hair was tied into a bundle pointing skyward. He looked as if he'd
just stepped off the set of a *kung fu* movie.

Aha! Finally. You're alive! You're alive! You're awake! I have waited for
three years, but you just kept snoring. How are you feeling?

Mr. Toan's throat was dry and sore. He tried to raise his head and open
his mouth, but he couldn't say anything.

He could make no sound.

The costumed man—probably a military mandarin—ordered someone
to drip water into Mr. Toan's mouth. Then he said, Hurry up. Hurry up.
You woke up just in time. This must be the sign that Heaven has agreed for
us to move the troops out. We have Heaven's blessing! We will give you a
title, or you can pick one for yourself. Your charge is to drive the emperor.
Northward! Northward!

The Toyota became the vehicle that would carry Emperor Quang Trung
to the north, to fight against northern invaders, soldiers of the Qing
emperor. Quang Trung's driver was to be Tran Toan, former tank commander and colonel in the Army of the Republic of South Viet Nam. The
car and convoy of horse carriages, chariots, carts, and elephants set out just
after midnight on the first day of the Year of the Rooster.

As usual, there was no moon during Tet. Mr. Toan turned on the lights,
charging ahead. In one day, he delivered the emperor to the fort and city of
Thang Long. The horses and elephants stayed right behind the car, surprising the enemy's troops and defeating them. It would become one of the
most glorious victories against any enemy—from the north, the west, the
east, or the south—in Vietnamese history.

Alas, the old officer wasn't to take part in, or to witness, the final triumphant battle.

The emperor himself beheaded the old officer during the first minutes
after the Toyota led the convoy into the fort of Thang Long.

In his driver's seat at that moment, Mr. Toan had a quick reflection.
History would come to record the lightning speed with which Emperor
Quang Trung had moved. To go from mountainous central Viet Nam to

the north at such speed could only be a miracle. In truth, that lightning speed was achieved by means of the Toyota's engine.

Emperor Quang Trung was in the back seat. The divine emperor could read the thought that had crossed Mr. Toan's mind and found it offensive.

The emperor drew his magic sword and, in one move, cut off the head of the seditious driver.

And yet history would be kind to the man who did not mean to be disdainful.

His anger spent, Emperor Quang Trung ordered his men to bury Mr. Toan with all the dignity and rites due a high-ranking military mandarin. He then issued a decree declaring the driver a loyal and accomplished servant of the court that he would establish in Thang Long. He gave the man a long title posthumously, Quan Tuong Xa Ich Hau Ba Tuoc, which had something to do with elephants and chariots and was the equivalent of baron.

Later, when communism had collapsed in Viet Nam, people would often mistake the headless bronze statue in the center of Ha Noi's central park as that of Lenin. Many statues of Lenin were pulled down by the masses when they were emancipated.

But the bronze statue had been erected three centuries before to honor the old tank commander, the Toyota driver who had lost his head while helping bring victory to Emperor Quang Trung.

Some twenty years after Mr. Toan disappeared, his wife—Vanna Thi Nguyen, by now an old woman—took her children to visit their homeland.

Vinh (or Victor), Cuong (or Cowen), Loan (aka Lou-Ann), and Tuan (aka Tony) were now middle-aged. In fact, it was the children who had suggested the trip: they wanted to give their mother a chance to visit their native soil. They brought along their own families: wives and kids born in America. They visited temples, mountains, monuments of all types, and countless caves and rivers. They were there to soak in all the renowned tourist and historical sites.

In Ha Noi, which had once been named Thang Long, they were taken to a special site. They had no way of knowing that this place had a direct link to their orphaned fate: that it had much to do with the extraordinary life of their father.

The place where they were taken was an exhibition hall with massive glass walls on all four sides. Inside were the latest and finest models of automobiles from one of the world's most famous manufacturers. The cars were polished so that they shone brightly under the neon lights.

Outside, there was a classy gray granite wall, equally polished. The large letters on the wall stood five feet tall. Together they read: TOYOTA CENTRAL DEALERSHIP, VIET NAM.

Each day, two workers cleaned and polished the bronze letters from early morning until customers began arriving. It was such an extraordinary site that the dealership was included in tours organized by the ministry of tourism: a must-visit by any and all who came to Ha Noi.

In the middle of the exhibition hall, Vinh, or Victor, marveled at a gold Toyota, slowly turning atop a massive marble pedestal.

The car was old, and Victor was approaching his fifties. His eyes weren't bad, but he could no longer recognize the revered object as a car he once owned, offered decades ago as a welcome gift to a father he barely knew. It had been the car that drew his father through a torrential river coursing through the rich and sorrowful history of a poor and unfortunate nation.

TONKIN

180 — HANOI - Pagode de l'Epée sur le Petit Lac

Catching Clams at Lake Isabella

A couple of weeks after our family came to the United States and settled in this town, Chung came to visit. A week before, there was Father Tue, who brought us a load of frozen meat wrapped in yellowed paper. Mother put it all in the fridge, and it took more than a week for us to discover that the load of precious food had gone a full year past its expiration date. Mother reluctantly put it all in the trash bin, still unable to forget the baskets of rotten fish that stank up our entire neighborhood in Saigon, near the state shop where people were always fighting each other. "Buddha be a witness," she said. "I won't speak ill of him. He was kind enough to bring us the food." Naturally, I said nothing. In our family, it was always the women who worried about such things.

Chung arrived without any packages of frozen meat, but he had a complete toolbox in the back of his gray pickup truck. He went around our one-bedroom apartment, empty of things but crowded with people, checking each electrical outlet, all the faucets in the bathroom, the gas oven, and the brand-new refrigerator, which my sister, who'd come to America years before, had bought for us. We all followed Chung and watched everything he did. One of us always had a quick and ready answer to his questions. Chung's first visit was enough to make my mother quite fond of him. "What a terribly nice man!" My wife turned a smile toward my unmarried sister, then said to my mother, "The guy's married with two kids, Mother." My sister was irritated. "Such a dark-skinned man. Who'd want him?" Mother ended the discussion with a rather fine proverb: "Indeed, it's soot sneering at charcoal!"

Chung and I quickly became friends. In my third week as a refugee, I got a humble job at a local restaurant. I would continue to find such humble jobs in the years following. On his days off, Chung called to invite me over, usually in the evenings. At his house, we sat at the dining table in the kitchen to drink beer and talk about our affairs and other people's. His wife never joined us on such occasions. She didn't speak Vietnamese. She replied to her husband's questions in the soft drawl of people from a southern state. She was an American woman half a head taller than Chung and quiet. She had a round, freckled face that seemed sadly peaceful, or peacefully sad, as if these two things necessarily went together. Later, I found out that Chung had worked hard for years supporting her while she studied for a nursing degree at the university west of our town. He continued to work hard after she graduated and found a job. A machinist, he seemed to be happy with his line of work. Even now, I still don't know how it was that the young American woman and the Vietnamese veteran came to be married. Chung never told me, and I never asked.

The town we lived in was set deep inside a flat valley that stretched for hundreds of miles. From the town, you could go in any direction and face vast fields and, far beyond, one mountain range after another. Once in a while, Chung would take me to the newly harvested fields. We would walk along the dirt banks, bending down to pick up stray garlic or onion bulbs and potatoes. We soon filled up plastic bags from Safeway or Von's and carefully tied them before putting them in the back of the gray pickup truck. We were always excited on our way back, so we didn't care about our faces and hands being dirty. On these occasions, Chung often recounted stories about finding yams and beans when he was young. He'd quickly clean the pieces of purple yam, not much longer than a small finger, and put them in his mouth, chewing loudly. "They were so sweet, my friend!" For some months afterwards, we went on such "harvest" trips, sometimes with a few Vietnamese friends from town. Chung's wife and kids never came with us. "They keep asking why I won't buy the vegetables at the supermarket since they don't cost much and it'd save time," Chung replied whenever someone asked about his family.

One day, Chung called, excited. "Come on over, I have something special." When I arrived, Chung was moving about in the kitchen, all alone. His wife and kids must have gone out shopping or something. He was grilling thin, flat rice cakes on the electric range. The "something special" was pungent with the smell of onion and garlic and lay steaming in a large porcelain dish on the dining table. It turned out to be fried oysters. "Where did you find such small oysters?" I asked. "They're not oysters. Clams," Chung answered in a firm voice. I didn't know there were clams around here. They were the size of your thumbnail and had shells the color of moss, the kind my mother often bought to make basil soup. It'd been a long time since I'd had any basil soup. There was no basil growing around here, and certainly no clams where we lived. I took a closer look at the black shells. These were baby clams. "Where did you find them?" "At a lake up in the mountains. We'll go up there sometime," Chung replied in the same firm voice.

Leaving behind the orchards, Highway 178 winds close to the upper part of Kern River, which the locals call The Killer River. From here, Highway 178 turns into a dangerous pass. The road narrows, the two-lane highway zigzags between the mountain on one side and, on the other, a cliff dropping down three hundred feet to the torrential river. Every few miles along the road, there is a space carved deep in the mountainside—or sitting precipitously on the edge of the cliff—where broken-down or slow-moving cars can stop to get out of the way of other cars. At the top of the pass, where the road ends, is Lake Isabella, once a natural valley at the foot of the tall mountains. Here, rainwater and snow melting each spring would collect before pouring into the upper part of Kern River in a colossal waterfall. The southern edge of the lake was hemmed in by a concrete dam, and at each end of the dam were large rocks from which gnarled trees grew. The lake was vast, and a pebbled path ran along its edge. On weekends, people from nearby towns went there to camp, fish, and water ski, turning the area into an active and noisy park.

It was to Lake Isabella that Chung and I drove to find clams. We stopped at a quiet part of the lake. Bringing along a small rake and canvas bags, we waded out to where the water came to our waists, then began digging and raking in the black mud. There were quite a lot of them, so our task wasn't that difficult. After just a few hours, the four bags were filled with small black clams. Chung threw them in the bed of his truck, and we set off excitedly. As we drove down the mountain pass, the cliffs on my side sometimes disappeared from view when we rounded the dangerous bends. I felt sick to my stomach. Down below, the Kern twisted and turned noisily between the steep mountainsides. Chung completely ignored my nervousness. Once in a while, he would take his eyes off the winding road and look into the rearview mirror. I assumed he was thinking of the baby clams—as he insisted they were—in the bags in the back of the pickup.

Chung never tired of repeating his stories about catching clams along the banks of Cai River. A newly dug river had robbed the Cai of its water, and it was drying day by day. In some places, the riverbed was just stretches of sand. Clams the size of thumbnails collected in the areas where the water came up to one's waist.

Chung was born in the central part of Viet Nam to a poor family. His father died early on, and his mother worked hard all her life to support the family. Chung was obsessed with the sandy roots of purple yams, the precious rice grains that had been dropped on the newly harvested fields, and the moss-colored clams in the shallow parts of the river. "Sometimes I'd catch mussels. I'd crack them open to look for pearls!" I laughed at the idea of there being any pearls in a mussel. "I was a kid then," Chung said, "real stupid. I was always thinking of the story of Trong Thuy and My Chau."

Our impoverished homeland has many legends. Almost any Vietnamese would know the story of how Trong Thuy's father, king of the Trieu kingdom, had sent him to the court of the Thuc to steal the magic bow that had thwarted his attacks time and again. Prince Trong Thuy married the Thuc princess My Chau, and they found much happiness in each other until Trong Thuy was able to swap the magic bow with a fake one and had to return home. "If anything happens and you need to flee your kingdom, leave traces so I can find you," Trong Thuy told the princess. Holding a down pillow to her chest, My Chau replied, "Follow the path with goose feathers and you'll always find me." The Trieu's next surprise attack was like a tempest. Casting away the useless bow, the Thuc king threw his daughter on the back of his horse and rushed away from the imperial city of Co Loa as it burned. In haste, Princess My Chau was only able to grab her goose-down pillow, upon which she had rested her head nightly to mourn the end of happy days with her husband. The soft goose feathers fell along the escape route. The Thuc king and his horse rested by a lake that poured into the sea. The lake was too big to cross, and then came the echoes of the Trieu's galloping horses. The king turned his head just as the last feather fell from the princess's hand. The escape route, littered with goose feathers, had shown the enemy the way. The Thuc king drew his sword on My Chau, and she fell down by the water's edge, her blood pouring into the big lake. The lake's oysters would embrace My Chau's drops of blood and mix them with the shiny liquid that turned into pearls. But that would happen later, long after Trong Thuy found his way there. A traitor always appears too late, but punishment sometimes comes quite early. People later said that pearls from the big lake would be more sparkling, more beautiful if they were washed with water that came from the well in Co Loa where Trong Thuy drowned himself after finding the princess. Perhaps the prince's decision to kill himself came from unbearable guilt or grief, or both. The pearls were taken to China, where emperors, princes, and princesses would have them sewn onto their courtly outfits for ceremonies and celebrations. There were no pearls for a boy looking for clams in the river running through a small village in central Viet Nam.

For a while, I continued to go with Chung to look for clams and for onion and garlic. Then life began to be burdensome. There were concerns more pressing than gathering baby clams from a man-made lake in the mountains. Work, daily necessities, and new problems in my marriage demanded time and attention. When I turned down Chung's invitation to go look for garlic, he couldn't hide his disappointment. "Isn't there anyone else who could go with you?" I asked. "They keep asking why I won't buy the vegetables at the supermarket, since they don't cost much and it'd save time." The occasions on which I joined Chung to go to Lake Isabella became rarer, and then I stopped going altogether. The disagreements between my wife and me seemed insurmountable. We finally decided that we would try to solve the problems separately. And so we said goodbye, taking with us the same problems without solutions and the sadness that came from our individual failures. Later, Chung occasionally visited my tiny apartment, bringing strands of garlic still covered in dust and sand, or clams still in their black shells. It seemed his wife and kids and his Vietnamese friends in town only wanted the garlic you buy at the supermarket. Even the tasty plates of clams fried with onion and lemongrass and the crispy rice cakes would be bland if you had to eat them by yourself.

I learned about the accident on the Highway 178 pass from the eleven-o'clock news on a local TV station. The gray pickup had fallen down a rocky cliff and sunk into the thrashing water of Kern River, scattering the bags full of small clams. "It was too late by the time the driver of the semi caught sight of the man at the back of his truck. The victim and the gray pickup were sent over the cliff's edge, falling down three hundred feet into Kern River, and were dragged downstream immediately by the forceful currents. All that was left was a long line of small oysters, smashed into smithereens by the wheels of the semi." The camera focused on the tarred road, and I could see the shattered shells. Nothing was said of the bags, which had fallen into the water with the pickup and the ill-fated man. "No one will ever know why this man had recklessly stopped around the dangerous bend, by a steep cliff just above the violent Kern River." That was how the television reporter ended his story. Believing I understood a little of what had happened, I couldn't agree with the reporter's account of the crash.

The canvas cover above the pickup's bed had somehow flown open, and the small clams from one of the bags had been scattered on the road. I can easily imagine Chung stopping his truck next to the precarious cliff to refasten the cover. He might have even tried to look, in the darkening light of the evening, for the clams that had spilled onto the bed of the pickup or onto the road. The TV reporter would never understand how someone could take such a risk just because of some worthless clams.

My homeland had no legends about clams. The bright-white pearls that came from My Chau's drops of blood and were worn on the outfits of emperors, princes, and princesses at ceremonies and celebrations had nothing to do with lowly clams, either in my homeland or in America. The ugly black clams from Chung's bags either would be smashed on the rocks in the river or would sink into the violent currents and be dragged downstream. A terrible journey for the pitiful clams. Some would get stuck among the rocks, others thrown out of the water, landing on stones and becoming food for hungry birds or otters. Luckier clams would continue downstream, where the current would slow down and pour into a big lake.

Surrounding Lake Isabella are pine, linden, and eucalyptus trees, which cast a cooling shadow over the sets of gray metal tables and chairs. On weekends, people gather here to spread their food on the long tables, sharing laughter and conversation over a meal and keeping an eye on the kids playing or swimming in the water. I come here too, sitting by myself on the stone bench by the lake, eating potato chips, watching my young daughters in their bright swimsuits chase graceless geese on the sandy shore. When they're through chasing, they rush into the lake, dipping themselves in the cooling water. Sometimes they go deep below the surface to search the bottom—perhaps to find a pebble of no particular shape, perhaps a single dark strand of grass. Sooner or later, they find what I want them to find. Then they rush up to stand around me, in their excitement fighting to talk to me. "Guess what we found." Of course I know. Daddy knows everything! "A goldfish," I answer, and they burst into laughter. "There's no goldfish in this lake. You can only find goldfish in the tanks in a Chinese restaurant—didn't you know that?" one of them reminds me. And the other carefully opens her small hand. "A baby oyster!" they shout in unison. I take the oyster into my hand to examine it for a while, and then I correct them. "No, this is a clam. It is called *hến*." Their tiny pink lips open, curl up, and twist around, and from them comes the word *hến*, sounding round and clear like the sound of a flute. The girls laugh loudly again. Pulling them to me, I turn toward the southeast, where a green mountain range sits in the afternoon sun. Lowering my voice as though about to unleash some deep secret, I tell them about the journey of the small clam in the palm of my hand—starting not from the high summit above Lake Isabella, nor from the steep cliff three hundred feet above the violent Kern River, but from a small village on the other side of the Pacific Ocean, where a passing river would, in time, dry up.

Translation by Nguyen Qui Duc

from *The Time Tree*

ASKING

I ask the earth: How does earth live with earth?
—We honor each other.

I ask water: How does water live with water?
—We fill each other up.

I ask the grass: How does grass live with grass?
—We weave into one another
  creating horizons.

I ask man: How does man live with man?
I ask man:
How does man live with man?
I ask man:
How does man live with man?

YOU

Someone wishes you dead,
But your breasts become more like precious jade each day.

Someone wishes infirmity upon you,
But your hair is black
And heaven comes down to watch
You wade through the mud
Alone
Shaking out your shirt,
Returning wind to the clouds.

Someone wishes you orphaned,
But you sing among low-flying dragonflies.

"Black clouds have gone to seal heaven's gates—
Young leaves hoping for someone's face after rain."

WINTER LETTER

The letter I wrote you had smeared ink,
But the bamboo walls are thin, and fog kept leaking through.
On this cold mountain, I cannot sleep at night.
By morning, a reed stalk can fade.

White snow on my thin blanket.
The stove glows red for lunch, but the mountain remains hazy.
Ink freezes inside my pen—
I hold it over the glowing coals and it melts into a letter.

Blocking the wind, a tree with purple roots trembles.
Corn seeds shrivel underground.
On days when my comrades are on assignment,
I miss them, but . . . there is an extra blanket.

The cold rooster crows lazily in a hoarse voice.
We beat on the cups, the bowls, to ease the strangeness.
The mountain hides hundreds of ores in its bosom.
I try, but can't find enough vegetables for a meal.

The rice often comes early, the letters late.
The radio is on all night to make the bunker seem less desolate.
So many years without seeing women,
I mistake the sound of horse hooves for your footsteps.

Gathering clouds often invite me to dream.
Very late, and you by a glowing light.
Wishing I had some scent of soapberry
So rocks would soften, the mountains grow warm.

Translations by George Evans and Nguyen Qui Duc

MAI THAO

Four Poems

BEYOND POETRY

Wake at midnight, the body stretched out,
read a friend's poem, other lines follow.
Lines of long ago, lines unceasing,
a glimpse of that distant shore.

ALONE

Alone like a statue in a corner,
Voice asks: What drink would you like?
Drink? I say. Bring me a gulp of the heart-tearing afternoon.
A bottle of darkness full to the brim.

SOUNDLESS

Leave early in the morning, the flowers know nothing.
Return late at night, the evening branches know nothing.
Only the moon sometimes catches a glimpse,
a stooped shadow moving along a darkened wall.

THE PAST

Sometimes departed spirits wake up inside me,
they set off wildfires and floods in my heart.
With great regret I have to tell them,
Too late, the grave is dug, grass grows over it.

Translations by Kevin Bowen and Nguyen Ba Chung

INDO-CHINE FRANÇAISE

CARTE POSTALE

Ce côté est exclusivement réservé à l'adresse

Monsieur Louis Sylvestre
47 Rue Monge
Paris V[e]

書紙會同帖
紙家號寄戶

Bons souvenirs, bonnes amitiés, bons baisers à Tous et à Toutes!!!

Ducey

Collection P. Dieulefils, Photographe, 53, rue Jules Ferry à Hanoi

3046. TONKIN — Baie d'Along - Rochers

Three Poems

POETRY MANIFESTO FOR THE NEW MILLENNIUM

Write poems always the martial arts for adventurers
Ossein, pills, and powder—hereditary family power

Poems especially to cure leprosy
Diabetes and bloody urination
V.D.
Skin diseases, irregular menstruation

Poems to beautify what's ugly
Poems to clean what's grimy
Poems to bring sight to the sightless

Now and a thousand years to come.

MAIN STREET REVISITED

Our parents and grandparents, directors of the stage
They play their trumpets and drums a bit poorly
That's to say it kindly
Before we can learn the four directions and how to count
They carry us on their backs south of the seventeenth parallel
Raise us up on sun-soaked boulevards
Under the shadows of ramrod-straight flaming trees
They, the directors of the stage
Of half of what no one could seriously call a country
They left behind the coins in their pockets
Boarded the helicopters that landed on the roofs
Steered their boats to the high sea

Now occasionally we return
Sing *karaoke* with girls half our age
Songs that our parents and grandparents, directors of the stage,
Worthless left behind

KRUNG THEP PRINCESS MINGLES BAR
MIDNIGHT BLUES

Put me up!
Put me down!
Put my feet back on the ground!

This woman is short but wears a miniskirt
A ten-centimeter heel couldn't make her legs any longer

She drains the life out of me with her singing

here at the dance hall, second floor of the hotel
Atrium, 1880 Pechtburi Bangkok.

Queen of the stage
queen of the blow-dried haircut
queen of the hot tub
queens who lie inviting

Twelve months multiplying in the sea
Gates big and small sit watching the tide

Queens hiding their heads under the table
Mouths chewing audibly
Queens of the streets

Les princesses!
Les princesses de la rue!

My queen
In the nightclub of a Ha Noi hotel
A short leg is like any short leg
Knees on the stage all look alike

Look at you, dancing body lustful
colored lights
One looks like the other
She raises her leg, her hand
Country roads, take me home!
Breaking heart! Aching heart!
Who will ever stop the rain . . .

And

This season there is no rain . . .

I feel sad to the point of tears
but not a drop comes
to fall into my orange vodka.

Obladioblada.

Translations by Kevin Bowen and Nguyen Ba Chung

2. SAIGON — Palais du Gouverneur de la Cochinchine

Coming Full Circle: A Conversation with Nguyen Duy

Nguyen Duy was born in 1946 in the village of Dong Ve in Thanh Hoa Province. He joined the local militia forces defending Ham Rong Bridge in 1963. From 1965 to 1975, he served as a signal soldier responsible for laying down communication lines for the field command in the South, where he covered and fought in most of the major campaigns, including those in Khe Sanh, Quang Tri, and Laos. As a response to the hardship and suffering at the front, he began writing poetry, and as his work came to be known, his poems were read over the radio. After the war, he settled in Ho Chi Minh City, where he became the southern editor for the literary journal *Van Nghe.*

Duy's settlement in the south was an important event that marked the creation of a milieu in which artists, writers, and musicians from north and south—including PAVN, NLF, and perhaps even ARVN forces—might support each other in creating new forums for the arts. Duy's heartfelt rendering of the hardships of country life as well as his critiques and sometimes searing assessments of urban post-war life and leadership won him a loyal following both in Viet Nam and abroad. Showing a mastery of traditional forms as well as free verse, his work continued to evolve through the late 1990s, when he traveled to the United States and Europe and collaborated with Vietnamese artists, choreographers, and musicians in programs that integrated various artistic forms. The author of over a dozen collections of poetry, he announced in 1997 that he would no longer write poems. In 2000, Curbstone Press published *Distant Road: Selected Poems of Nguyen Duy,* a bilingual collection.

The following conversation was conducted in Vietnamese on 25 August 2001. In it, Duy makes a distinction between the phrase *o nuoc ngoai* (live abroad) and *hai ngoai* (overseas). The phrase *o nuoc ngoai* is less of a divisive term than *hai ngoai,* as it, by denotation as well as connotation, indicates Vietnamese who live outside of Viet Nam, whether voluntarily or involuntarily. *Hai ngoai* (overseas), a phrase of Sino-Vietnamese origin, is virtually identical in meaning but indicates those who have to go overseas under duress.

NC   The village and village life have occupied such a prominent place in your poetry, not as an abstract idea, but as something very concrete, very alive that people can almost smell, touch, and know. Recently, you made that connection between village life and your poetry even more explicit in a "poetry exhibit" that showed in Ha Noi, Thanh Hoa, and Ho Chi Minh City. It was probably the first event of its kind: poems living side by side with the most common artifacts of village life—well-worn bamboo baskets, old carrying poles, jute mats, earthen pots, and so on. Do you think that the youth of today still hold such a deep attachment to the village?

ND   Time changes, and with it come the changes to all the material and spiritual needs all of us have. The global video and audio culture—with its advanced technology, its worldwide distribution via radio, TV, CDs, DVDs, internet—has crossed national borders. Viet Nam's young generation cannot be an exception. The traditional village culture of Viet Nam is an important factor in what it means to be Vietnamese and is being more and more overshadowed every day. But since it has been so much and so long a part of the national culture, it has become almost hereditary and therefore cannot be easily eroded. It somehow remains, continuing its flow through the veins, and makes itself an indispensable part of Vietnamese poetry. This is true, in a way, with every culture.

NC   You have had many poetry readings, from Asia to Europe and the United States. What is the place of poetry in the world? How do you find people react to Vietnamese poetry?

ND   Poetry is the language of the soul. In this sense, there is equality among poets all over the world. The poetry of one place might be different from that of another because it's imbued with the scents and flavors of its place of origin. It's a fact that the world knows very little, in some cases nothing at all, about Vietnamese poetry. But because poetry has played such an important role in Vietnamese history, "Viet Nam" is, in a way, the name of a poem, not a war. I believe that with good translation and better dissemination, Vietnamese poetry will be better known and appreciated. The recent success of the collection of Ho Xuan Huong's poems, *Spring Essence,* is an example.

NC   You have been to the United States three times—in 1995, 2000, and 2001—and you've traveled even more often to Europe. You have had extensive contact with members of the Vietnamese overseas communities. What do you think of the Vietnamese poetry overseas? Its perambulations from 1975 to today? What do you see as the future of this poetry? Will there be a kind of hyphenated poetry—half Vietnamese and half English, half French, half German—or all English or French or German down the road?

ND The Vietnamese who *o nuoc ngoai* (live abroad)—pardon me, I do not like the term *hai ngoai* (overseas)—still write poetry, and most of them continue to write it only in Vietnamese. Each language has its own spirit. You can change the words, the phrases, the pronunciations, but you cannot easily change the spirit. So the writers who live abroad continue to write in Vietnamese. As for a marriage of languages, I cannot imagine a hyphenated poetry—half Vietnamese and half English or some other language. Poetry can't be created via bi-national marriages or artificial insemination. There might be first-class Vietnamese scientists of the first generation, but it's doubtful there could be first-class Vietnamese poets in the English, French, or German language so soon. There may well be such poets down the road; but it'll take some time, at least a generation, for the cultural heritage to be replaced and its spirit reoriented.

NC Poetry, as you have mentioned earlier, has played such a central role in Vietnamese culture. With the advent of industrialization, modernization, and globalization, can it hold on to this prominent place?

ND You can see that it's slipping right now. Perhaps it will slip even more down the road. But things have a way of coming full circle: the time for poetry will return, and not just in Viet Nam either.

NC During the last half century, the war has been the central subject of Vietnamese poetry. What has been its impact on your poetry and the writings of your generation? Now that Viet Nam has finally achieved peace, what are the concerns of today's poets?

ND The principal themes of poetry are always people, their lives, and their struggles in their particular environments. My generation had been submerged in war; war was therefore an integral part of our writing. But if we let time-bound factors completely dominate, there won't be any poetry.

NC During the 1930s, Vietnamese poetry broke away from its millennium-old moorings with the arrival of the New Poetry movement. Then came the August Revolution in 1945 and the predominant presence of Revolutionary Poetry. Do you see a need now for another breakaway: a poetry for the contemporary period? Could Vietnamese poets living abroad make contributions to this poetry?

ND The "new" in poetry isn't the same as the "new" in fashion or fad. When it's new, it appears of its own accord. It can neither be produced on order nor prohibited on order. What's new in poetry results from the coming together of what's new in the individual's spirit and the spiritual life of the time. Vietnamese poets living abroad can act as a bridge between Vietnamese poetry and world poetry. It's a contribution befitting the circumstance of the time. But whether contemporary Vietnamese poetry can create a new departure is something that will be determined by poets living in the homeland. I can sense that this departure has already begun. It will neither stop nor be stopped.

NC In 1997, you announced that you'd no longer write poetry. Could you tell us the reasons behind that surprising and extraordinary decision?

ND I started writing poems when I was in elementary school. I got my first poem published in 1967, when I was in the army. With the arrival of 1997, I had spent thirty years of my life writing poetry and had released thirteen collections of poems—many published in anthologies. I had always tried to not repeat myself with any poem, any idea, any line. Unfortunately, I'm getting older every day, and can feel the calcification of my feelings. My lines haven't become a stagnant pool, but there are signs that they may be revolving like a muddy current. I think there is nothing more frightening than to have to listen to someone who keeps repeating himself. I would want to do something different, something new, but it isn't easy. Writing a poem is not like making an object. If an oil well has dried up, one had better stop pumping and start looking for another.

NC Have you recently seen any poet in Viet Nam who has been able to say something new—newer than what Nguyen Duy has said?

ND Different, yes—sometimes even wickedly different. Really new? Not yet, but I'm sure that it will happen.

NC Now that you no longer write poems, are you still pursuing your literary interests?

ND The fact that I stopped writing poetry doesn't mean that I broke off from poetry. Poetry is my vocation, my life. In a way, I still "write" poetry by reading, reciting, printing, exhibiting poetry, publishing poetry calendars while searching for a new poetic well. And while waiting for some undefinable, heaven-sent well, I still like to write something—prose, for example. Something about my native village, my childhood, love and war. My immediate need is to make enough to take care of the basic needs of my family. I have a big family, with serious health problems. That's the reason I decided to go into the business of publishing calendars: calendars "exhibiting" poetry.

NC Clearly you are the creator of this new kind of calendar. You started in 1999 and have been extremely successful at it, both artistically and financially. Are the satisfactions—artistic and financial—similar in any way?

ND Writing poetry isn't a profession, a career. In Viet Nam, perhaps as elsewhere, the poet has to survive and support poetry by taking up some other means of making a living—including being supported by somebody else. "O poetry, I'll give you my word / I'll plow / and plant long and hard to keep you alive" ["Subsidized Poetry"]. Poetry cannot be a business, but publishing poetry is a legitimate business. To me, publishing a poetry calendar is an effective way to introduce poetry to a great number of people —inside as well as outside Viet Nam. But it's not an easy game. There are many difficulties, the largest of which is finding good poetry. It's rare to find good poems, and yet people would not pay for bad ones.

NC In your poetry, there are three figures that stand out: Grandmother, Mother, and Father. Could you let us know the influence of your loved ones on your poetry? Of loved ones on the poetry of Viet Nam in general?

ND The family bond is the premier relationship in the East in general and in Viet Nam in particular. Grandparents and parents have been progenitors, educators, and economic supporters for centuries in Viet Nam. Through the self-subsistent local economy and the village's tradition of "like father like son," the elders put their deepest imprints on each one of us—especially on those who aspire to write, for writers are vampires feeding on the mother tongue and the people's soul.

Translation by Nguyen Ba Chung

Mad Dog: The Legend of
Chinese Poet Guo Lusheng

Fifty men in pajamas crowd the common room of a mental institution in Beijing. Some sit shoulder to shoulder on the concrete floor with their backs against the wall. Others watch television or wander about, talking to themselves, lost in worlds of their own. One patient stands apart, smoking and staring through the barred windows to the garden below. Hair cropped short, dressed in regulation pajamas, he looks like every other inmate; but this man's inner world may be more extraordinary than that of all the rest. He has been called China's Dante.

Respected then reviled by the Red Guards in the 1960s, later praised as the forerunner of the underground literature movement, criticized by the authorities, and recently back in favor enough to be published and to receive literary awards, fifty-two-year-old Guo Lusheng has been scarred by his journey through Maoist hell and by the mental breakdown caused in part by political persecution. But this poet is also a survivor and takes a calm view of the ups and downs in his life and the transient nature of fame. Tall and well built, he chain-smokes as we sit together at one of the greasy dining tables in Beijing's Social Welfare House No. 3. His face is expressive as he tells me about his life.

Guo Lusheng was born on a roadside in Shandong Province, southeast of Beijing, on a bitter winter's day in 1948. Civil war was raging across China. His father was in Mao's army, and his mother, like the wives of other soldiers, was traveling with the troops. The name they gave their infant, Lusheng, means "born on the road." Perhaps they felt that this inauspicious beginning meant that their son had a bumpy journey ahead of him.

Guo Yunxuan recalls that his son loved to read from the time he was little, and at three could already recite many classical poems, taught to him by his mother. "And he was stubborn," his father adds, "always had his own views on things."

An independent mind and love of books are admired in democratic cultures, but in the intensely politicized society of Mao's China, these qualities got Guo into trouble as soon as he was old enough to attend school. "When the Cultural Revolution came, I was very excited at first," Guo says as he recalls his youthful enthusiasm for revolutionary politics. His early poems were popular with his schoolmates. Ironically, they might have been too well known: Guo's undoing was brought about by an admiring teacher who wrote a mandatory "self-criticism" in which he admitted that he loved Guo's writing because it displayed "bourgeois" taste. After that, Guo and his poetry were spurned by the zealous Red Guard factions. When the Cultural Revolution intensified, all schools and universities were shut down. Forced to stay home, Guo began to meet other writers. Among these new friends were writers whose work was also criticized by the Red Guards and who were part of an underground literary salon called Sun Fleet.

"They were mostly children of the social elite," Guo remembers. "They had access to classic foreign books and even Beatles albums, which were unobtainable for ordinary people." Guo's friends opened his eyes to experiences that ranged from drinking and partying to earnest but secret discussions about literature and the future of China. Nonetheless, he was lucky not to have been admitted into formal membership of Sun Fleet. In 1966, the group was labeled a "counterrevolutionary" organization and its leader, Zhang Langlang, received a death sentence that was later suspended. Red Guards attacked several of Guo's friends, driving some to commit suicide. Even the son of China's poet laureate, the communist official Guo Moruo, was targeted because he led an underground literary group; captured, he was tied to a chair and thrown from a building to his death.

Though Guo escaped being labeled a counterrevolutionary, his association with Sun Fleet meant that the eighteen-year-old poet was branded a "rightist student" and given a permanent black mark in his all-important personal file. Terrified by the danger swirling around him, he nevertheless continued to write, producing such important early poems as "Believe in the Future." The poet Li Hengjui, a contemporary of Guo's, remembers being deeply moved the first time he read the poem. "I knew instantly that it was a masterpiece that needed to be distributed widely," Li says. Others felt the same, and the poem was disseminated at a remarkable speed, despite the limited means of transmission and the perils posed for those who had copies. At the time, Madame Mao held a fierce grip on the arts and permitted only eulogies to her husband to be published; a work like Guo's could not possibly be printed. And so the poem was copied out by hand and passed among friends who could be trusted.

"After Chairman Mao dumped us Red Guards, the movement went downhill," says Lin Mang, now a top literary critic and a famous poet. To curb Red Guard excesses, Mao began packing the young radicals off to the countryside, getting them out of the way and having them learn from the peasants. There, as elsewhere, many of the radical youths read Guo's work and found that it captured the pain and hope of an entire generation. "The tone of the poems is gray and heavy, which matched our mood," Lin adds. "But there is something beautiful and uplifting in it that offered spiritual sustenance." Li Hengjui, who was held in solitary confinement for ten years as a counterrevolutionary, says, "I could have gone mad in that three-meter-square room with no books or anything. It was Lusheng's poems that kept me going."

Before Guo's exile to the countryside in 1968, he found himself writing love poems. He had become infatuated with a beautiful Uygur girl, a Muslim Xinjiang named Lili, whose father was a central-government official. "I knew there was no hope, so I wrote several sad and beautiful poems to express my desperation," says Guo. At that time, love poems could not be found anywhere in printed form because they were considered counterrevolutionary and the authors were subject to punishment.

Guo was sent to Apricot Village, located in a poor rural area in central Shanxi Province. "My two years at Apricot Village were a very happy time," he recalls with his ready smile. "For the first time, I felt equal to everyone, without any political burden." After a hard day of tilling the land, the "sent-down youth"—those exiled to the countryside—would sing and read the precious books they had brought from home. "The most enjoyable thing," recalls Jiao Yuanchao, one of the other young students banished from Beijing to Apricot Village, "was listening to Lusheng read poems and tell stories."

After his stint in the countryside, the twenty-three-year-old Guo joined the People's Liberation Army. "I had always wanted to be a soldier," he says today. "And I thought if I could become a Party member, I would be able to get my poems published." Better educated and more experienced than the other recruits, Guo quickly acquired a clerical position. But in just over a year, this vital young poet, who had always been lively and optimistic, became withdrawn and depressed. "I doubt that any free-spirited man like Lusheng could survive in a strictly controlled, oppressive place like the army," speculates fellow writer Li Hengjui. Guo's father suspects that life in the army was made even more intolerable for his son because of the black mark in his personal file. He says, "The political instructor of his company told me he was a 'pink' poet—not 'red' enough to be a Party member."

Discharged early, Guo returned to Beijing and began the lowest period of his life. Most of his friends were trapped in either the countryside or the army. He shut himself in his room, ate little, and chain-smoked day and night. "I just felt totally lost and miserable," he recalls. Then one day his father noticed that he had drawn a picture of a man holding a long knife to his neck. "We began to worry he was going to commit suicide, so finally we took him to a mental hospital." Guo's father sometimes blames himself for not noticing his son's symptoms earlier, but more often he blames China's repressive society for his son's condition. "He always tried hard at school, down in the countryside, and in the army. But he simply could not get anywhere!" he says. Guo explains simply, "It was Chairman Mao who drove me mad."

After a few months of treatment, Guo was released from the hospital and assigned a janitor's job at the Beijing Photo-electricity Research Institute. Soon afterwards, he met Ala Li, the daughter of an aristocratic Russian woman and Li Lisan, China's former minister of labor, who had been a rival of Chairman Mao and had died under mysterious circumstances early in the Cultural Revolution. Guo fell in love with Ala, and the two were married after only a few months of courtship.

In the late seventies, after the death of Mao and the downfall of the Gang of Four, including Madame Mao, a more liberal attitude prevailed in the Party leadership, resulting in a golden age for unofficial publications. Writers were allowed to print and distribute their works without going through government printing houses. While literary works published in such official journals as *People's Literature* clung to the style approved of by the Cultural Revolution, the unofficial poetry scene was vibrant and experimental.

For a few brief months in 1978 and 1979, and amid the ragtag posters of the Democracy Wall movement, poets and writers gave eloquent expression to the suffering and terror that had been caused by the Cultural Revolution. Significant breakthroughs in poetry appeared in such unofficial magazines as *Exploration* (edited by Wei Jingsheng), *Beijing Spring,* and *Today,* the first underground poetry journal to be established in China. *Today*'s founding poets, Bei Dao and Mang Ke, were both keen admirers of Guo's work. When they asked him to contribute, he happily agreed. "We wanted to publish the underground literature that had been written during the Cultural Revolution," says Mang Ke. "He was just the best poet of the period, and his poems suited *Today*'s liberal and modern style very well."

"I am grateful to *Today,* through which I made some lifelong friends," says Guo. "Also, it was only because of *Today* that my poems were published." In addition to Guo's early works, the editors printed his newer compositions, such as "Mad Dog: To Those Who Indulge in Talks of Human Rights."

"That poem is my favorite," he says, "not only because it is kind of a self-portrait, but also because it's about the way that the character of the Chinese people has been distorted. People say one thing and do another. Being truthful to yourself is the basic human right."

It was during this period that Guo began to use his pen name, Shi Zhi, which means "index finger." He explains that a poet living in China faces huge pressures and that people often point at such a person and talk about him or her.

In 1982, Guo and Ala Li were divorced and his mental health, which had been fragile since 1973, quickly deteriorated. The death of his beloved mother six years later aggravated his decline, and it was soon after this that his retired father felt the need to take him to Social Welfare House No. 3, the mental ward in Changping County. His friends occasionally wrote articles about him, and there were even invitations to attend poetry conferences in London and Rotterdam. But he was unable to attend such events.

In 1993, Guo reemerged. By the time he and poet friend Hei Dachuan jointly published a book, he had already begun to acquire cult-like status. Adding significantly to his work's reputation and accessibility was the 1998 publication of his collected poems by the prestigious Writers' Publishing Company, made possible in part by his friend Lin Mang, a senior editor with China's Writers' Association and *Poem* magazine. "This genius poet should not be buried. He deserves a place in the history of poetry," explains Lin. "During the Cultural Revolution, so few real poems were written, but Guo's poems can stand the test of time. He was the forerunner of modern poetry in China. His poems have an independent and free spirit. Although *menglongshi* (Misty Poetry) came after the Cultural Revolution and is more modern in style, it carries the spirit that he initiated. Lusheng is indeed China's premier modern poet."

The first edition of six thousand copies of Guo's collection, *Poems of Shi Zhi,* sold well. And in spring 2001, the collection won him No Third People's Literature Award, a considerable honor for a Chinese writer. Those of Guo's generation found nostalgia in his poems; those of the younger generation, confronted by modern-day China's spiritual void, found that his poems had a refreshing, indomitable faith in the validity of personal truths. Recently, Guo's poems have even been printed in several authoritative anthologies, such as *Selected Poems of the Past 50 Years.* "Lusheng deserves it," says Li Hengjui. "As time goes by, people will appreciate his poems more and more. If his works had been translated into English, he could have won the Nobel Prize—not Gao Xingjian. He is China's Dante."

Cocooned in an institution, Guo is barely affected by his returning fame. He still shares a small room with four other inmates. He eats simple meals and smokes the cheapest brand of cigarettes. His "work unit" covers his medical costs, and his family pays for his food. Trying to be helpful in his ward, he mechanically sweeps the floor and washes dishes. "Of course, I hate the institution," he says. "Every day, I sit in the big common room with a bunch of loonies, watched over by doctors and nurses. I'm not allowed to read books. And this terrible environment leaves me longing for beautiful things. I believe that when your bitterness reaches its peak, your soul becomes perfect." But he adds, "If I can read, write, and think, I am content."

From time to time, one of Guo's fellow inmates will burst into the dining room, remarking with obvious envy, "You have visitors?" "I am very lucky," he says with a broad smile. "I have by far the largest number of visitors." Several times a year, his family picks him up for a brief return home. And his loyal friends always throw a big birthday party for him that is attended by poets, writers, and artists. Guo recognizes that his condition means he no longer fits into the so-called normal life back in the city. His dream is to have an apartment attached to the institution so that he will have more freedom as well as easy access to medical care. He also believes a little more independence will revive his flagging chances of remarriage. "When I wrote the poem 'Believe in the Future,' it was meant more for self-encouragement. Today, even in my poor state, I still see the beauty of life and believe in the future more than ever! Otherwise, what is the meaning of life?"

In the stark reception room of the mental ward, Guo rises to begin a recital. He stands tall and with great dignity, his hands moving excitedly in the air, as if he is facing a large audience. The noises and screams from the nearby common room are drowned out by his powerful, husky voice.

> *When spider webs seal my stove without mercy*
> *When ember smoke sighs over sad poverty*
> *I spread out the despairing ashes stubbornly*
> *And write with fair snowflakes: believe in the future*

Editor's note: The following poems by Shi Zhi were translated by Michelle Yeh.

AT THE MENTAL HOSPITAL

For poetry I'd search the whole wide world
But how can one meditate in the noisy ward
Plenty of ribald jokes and witty words
Yet I can't write a single line of verse

Sometimes I feel like venting my rage
But am cowed by what will come about
Heavens! Why do you time and time again
Make me waste my life in a crazy house!

. . . .
. . . .
. . . .
. . . .

When the roaring tide in my heart subsides
Only emptiness and sorrow will reside
Afraid that others may see my tearful eyes
I pace with my head low as if nothing to hide

(1991)

DESTINY

A good name is a bill too large to break,
A bad name is a cangue you cannot shake;
If such is the true way of the world,
I'd rather drift at sea forever.

But where can one find a sturdy raft?
I roam the streets without a home,
Hoping to knock on a friendly door,
To receive what little is my own.

My life is a tumbling withered leaf,
My future is a grain never to sprout;
If such is the true destiny for me,
I'd rather sing for brambles wild and stout.

Who cares if the thorns pierce my heart,
Fiery blood burns as if in flame,
Finding its way into rivers and lakes,
The man dies, but the spirit remains.

(1967)

MAD DOG: TO THOSE WHO INDULGE
IN TALKS OF HUMAN RIGHTS

After my share of cruel abuse,
I no longer see myself as human;
With a mad dog I am confused,
Wandering about in the world.

But I am not yet a mad dog,
No hunger and cold expose me to risks.
For this I wish I were a mad dog,
To feel more sharply survival's fists.

Yet I am less than a mad dog!
A dog can jump over the high wall,
But I only suffer without a word,
More sorrow for me than for a mad dog.

If I really turn into a mad dog,
These invisible chains I will fight.
And I won't hesitate to discard
What you call the sacred human rights.

(1978)

MY LAST BEIJING

This is Beijing at four-o-eight—
An ocean of tumbling hands;
This is Beijing at four-o-eight—
A long, glorious whistle.

The tall buildings of the station
Tremble all of a sudden;
Shocked, I look out the window
Wondering what is going on.

A spasm of pain shoots through my heart—it must be
Mama piercing it with her button-sewing needle and thread.
At this moment my heart turns into a kite;
The other end of the cord is in Mama's hand.

The cord is so taut it is about to break;
I have to thrust my body out of the window.
Then, only then do I realize
What is going on.

—The roaring tide of farewells
Is pushing the station off the ground;
Underneath my feet, Beijing
Is moving slowly.

Once again I wave at Beijing.
I want to grab her collar
And shout out loud:
"Remember me forever, Mama Beijing!"

At last I've grasped something.
Who cares whose hand it is—I won't let go!
For this is my Beijing,
This is my last Beijing.

(1968)

BELIEVE IN THE FUTURE

When spider webs seal my stove without mercy
When ember smoke sighs over sad poverty
I spread out the despairing ashes stubbornly
And write with fair snowflakes: believe in the future

When my purple grapes melt into dew in deep autumn
When my fresh bouquet is embraced in another bosom
I grasp a piece of vine withered and frozen
And write on the desolate earth: believe in the future

With my fingers like waves tumbling toward the sky
With my palm like the sun-lifting ocean tide
I wield the warm pen of the first morning light
And write with a child's hand: believe in the future

Why do I believe in the future with such tenacity
For I believe in the future humanity
She has eyelashes that pierce the stormy history
And irises that read the chapters of days gone by

As for our putrid flesh, the regrets of losing
Our way and the pains of failing, whether winning
People's moving tears and profound sympathy,
Or their jesting smiles and bitter sarcasm,

I believe they will cast a warm-hearted,
Objective, and fair judgment on our countless
Explorations, detours, failures, and successes
Yes, I wait for their judgment anxiously

My friend, believe in the future without doubt
Believe in persevering efforts
Believe in death-conquering youth
Believe in the future, cherish life

(*Beijing, 1968*)

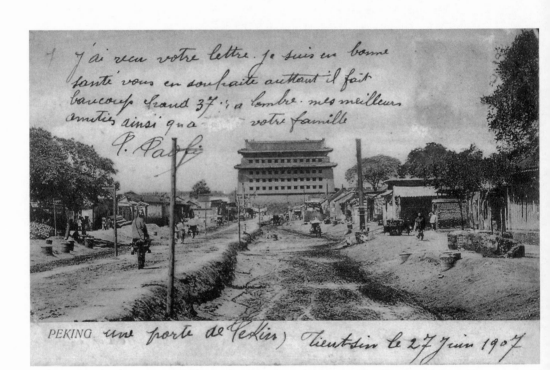

PEKING *une porte de Pekin) Tientsin le 27 Juin 1907*

from *Mount Paektu*

THE BATTLE

it was a long long fight
in the midst of the fight
I thought I caught a glimpse of my son, Pa-u
there wasn't even a moment to call him—*Pa-u!*
the battle was unrelenting
in the dark
I could get shot from either side
get stabbed by knives
get hit by rifle butts and fall
Japanese bombs exploded behind us
machine guns spilled out fire
inside the darkness
a mix of screams, cries
inside the darkness
knives collided with knives
the battle inside the darkness
lit up brightly for a second
then darkness again
there were only screams
over here, over there
am I fighting?
are you fighting?
are you an enemy or one of us?
in the end I kept pulling the trigger
it was daybreak
the fight ended as the sun rose
the sun rose to unveil
the men fallen on the battleground
50 independence fighters dead
100 or so injured
at times they were carried back on stretchers

some were dragged
some crawled
Pa-u, who got shot in the arm,
felt as if he were dead even though he was alive
he got dragged like that to the station for the injured
the violent fight has ended
the independence fighters won because
Song Sang-yong's raiding unit was in charge at the end
not all the corpses of Korean fighters were taken away
the bodies of Japanese soldiers mingled
with the bodies of independence fighters
when you die blood stops, blood hardens

MOUNT MIL

we went inside a shabby house
a couple took a room by themselves
so men and men
glued together
closed their eyes
endured the cold with little heat left over
our bodies didn't itch
maybe even the lice were dead
no
the men fell asleep not knowing the lice were busy
how long did we sleep?
like coming back from the dead
when we awoke
it was already pitch dark
the middle of the night
no water to moisten our throats
we closed and opened our eyes
listening to the wind outside
what were we thinking by coming all the way here?
even Kim T'u-man
was weary
looked back at his life up to then
when you turn your head to the past
even today
is not today
even tomorrow
even tomorrow
isn't a dream you'd run out to greet in your bare feet
the night was almost over then a glimpse of light
the door flung open

a Japanese policeman holding a rifle with a bayonet
a Jap!
all the way here
at the end of the world
behind him were spies
a Korean, also a Manchurian
more despicable than thieves
the Manchurian spy was about to approach
but the policeman told the Korean spy to step forward
"who are you all?"
the spy addressed us in harsh, rude language
Kim T'u-man stepped out, blocking Tol-sok
our first worry was the gun aimed at us
Almost servile, Kim T'u-man answered
"yes, yes, we are on our way to Moktan River or to Imku
we'll farm if we can
if not
we'll do whatever we must
to be able to put a morsel of food in our throats
in Korea we are nothing but peasants
so we own nothing
we heard that if we went to Manchuria we would be well off
but when we arrived in Yongture
all the land was already taken
so we tried coming out this far"
"is that so?
aren't you those worthless independence fighters?"
Kim T'u-man put on a straight face and replied,
heartbreakingly sincere,
"what, independence fighters?
we aren't even the in-laws of those fighters
if we have only two meals a day
I suppose that could make us independence fighters
but from what I heard
more fighters are dying from starving and freezing
than from fighting"
the Korean spy
interpreted for the Japanese policeman
then the spy seemed more relaxed and turned to us
"my father was a member of the pro-Japanese committee
but he was beaten to death by another Korean
I've come to find the fighters
to avenge my father's death
give me your word you'll tell me
if you ever come across them or anyone else"

Kim T'u-man bowed and said
"of course"
but the spy had more to say
"what do these fighters do anyway?
just a few fighters
they think they can reclaim a nation?
no way
Japan is the country that beat China
even Russia
you said you really weren't
those worthless fighters?"
Kim T'u-man cowered and answered
"how can we be those wretched men?
never mind being the fighters
even if we were told to we couldn't pretend
to be the grandfathers of the fighters
all we want is to farm and fill our bellies"
at that moment, the Japanese policeman
looked over every inch of Kim T'u-man
then he turned his gaze to Tol-sok
and stared him down for a while
but when Tol-sok coughed harshly
yellowish slime came out of his nose
"let's go!"
the policeman said in disgust
he patted the Korean spy and left
the spy said for the last time
"from now on
you must all report everything bad to me—
understand me?"

Translations by Don Mee Choi

485. TONKIN — Sontay - Porte Est, Citadelle

Collection P. Dieulefils, 53, Rue Jules-Ferry - Hanoi

from *War Child* _____

We didn't see much of the war between the North and the South, though it was never far away. The war was on the other side of the canal, over the hills in the mountains and jungle. We never saw the battles or the skirmishes in the swamps and paddies. To us the war was the distant thunder of howitzers, the shudder of our bungalow door, the helicopter blades whipping the air. The war was green and yellow star clusters flaring across the moonless skies, the prison searchlights, and the air-raid sirens. It was the sand-filled burlap bags of the bomb shelter and the faces of strangers springing from the dark under the lantern light. The war was the muffled reports of assault rifles somewhere in the jungle, the cadences of soldiers marching through the streets of Da Nang. The war was orange-robed monks leading funeral processions through streets littered with the fresh dung of oxen.

Sometimes the war was sticks of incense burned for prayer, sometimes olive-green tin cans of C-rations labeled with black stars. Sometimes the war was canisters of spilled chemicals and sun-blistered barrels of tar in the slums and shantytowns where we lived. But the war was mostly news over the radio and stories overheard from our neighbors. Stories of the death of a son, father, or distant cousin. Stories like the ones my mother told of how our fathers died. I imagined what must have happened to my father as my mother told neighbors her version of the story. While my mother and her friends drank tea in the afternoons and read the veins of tea leaves held over candles to tell their fortunes, I saw my father crossing a bridge over a narrow river. I saw the hump of the rucksack on his back, his ammo clips, and his rifle. I imagined the pineapple grenade arcing in the sky and bouncing on the wooden planks of the bridge. Then my mother would tell the story of how Sa's father died: how he had run from an exploding helicopter on a landing zone and how a rotor blade had cut off his head.

We never knew for sure if the stories were true, but we knew our fathers died the deaths of heroes. Sometimes we thought our fathers were still alive, that they walked the streets of Da Nang, that they would pull up in a jeep or jump out of a helicopter that landed nearby. We wanted to find our fathers. We often searched the faces of the soldiers patrolling the streets and sometimes we mistook a client for a father. Whenever my brother and I got our mother alone, we asked her about our fathers. We asked her about them during the typhoons that trapped us in our bungalow.

Once during a typhoon, our mother lit sticks of incense to pray to the Buddha, and my brother asked her if she had pictures of his father. She shook her head and knelt down and prayed for our safety. Though she said no, we always wondered if she had the photographs. We wondered if she hid them in a footlocker given to her by one of her clients. She kept it locked up in a far corner of the bungalow and was careful to guard its contents from our eyes. It was full of secrets. As the typhoon winds ripped up the corrugated tin roofs of the shantytown, flung the roofs like paper into the air, and whipped the rain against our door, we begged our mother to let us see what was in the locker. When our begging failed, we asked her questions about our fathers and questions about America.

"What did he look like?" we asked her as the typhoon winds howled and water seeped under the door.

But her answers were always brief, and she pretended to be busy counting her bills and coins and stuffing them in empty tea boxes stacked up against the bungalow wall that faced the Buddha.

After the typhoons passed, Ma ventured out and left us to ourselves. My brother and I emerged from the bungalow, excited about the flooding and the wreckage. We played in the retreating waters of the flooded dumps. We surfed on broken doors, floating in the knee-deep waters. We forgot about our fathers, forgot about America until we came back home and saw a client leaving our bungalow. I liked the typhoons because my mother stayed home with us. The clients were absent, and without them it was just the three of us waiting out the storms.

If we needed a new adventure to escape our bungalow walls, we ran to the market, where we were known for being thieves. We ran across the rain-washed sandstone of the temple grounds, ran through our city of siren speakers strapped on bomb shelters. We ran through streets shaded by the high walls of French residences and ran past camouflaged artillery pieces. We ran by the shantytown's rusty fences of tin cans and shacks ripped apart by typhoons and through our city of coconut palms and banana fronds, and in the dry season, we ran through hot air fragrant with tomato plants. Sometimes we stopped at the Town Square to watch the table-tennis players, blurred hands slapping Ping-Pong balls back and forth over the nets of the green tables.

But we never stayed in one place for very long. We were always on the run for one reason or other—mostly because we were thieves. We stole fishing line and rubber bands from the French shop owner. We lifted fruit from the market stands whenever we were hungry. Once, my brother stole a soldier's field cap as it rested on a restaurant table, and we escaped by disappearing into the shuffling crowds of the market.

Early one evening, we ran through the intersection where the shoeshine boys and girls called to pedestrians and the orange robes of the monks billowed like flames as they walked down the streets holding wooden bowls and begging for rice. People dressed in burlap bags squatted on the corners begging for food and coins. I saw one with a lump on his throat the size of a mango. My brother wanted to steal the coins in his bowl. The traffic picked up, and dust rose in a haze over the intersection. Vendors pushed their carts off to the side of the streets. Some of them were chipping blocks of ice, and others used machetes to chop up rods of sugarcane and hack the tops off coconuts to make iced drinks as their customers waited patiently.

A few days later, I felt a lump on my throat, which grew bigger as the days passed until it was the size of a fig. I was frightened. I was very superstitious, so I thought that I had caught the beggar's disease.

"Will I have to beg?" I asked my mother.

"Beg for what?" she said.

"Beg on the streets," I said, remembering the man in his ragged clothes, his hands clutching the lump on his throat.

"What do you mean?"

"The beggar on the street has a lump on his throat, and now I do, too."

"Dung, all you've got is a boil. We'll pop it when it's ready," my mother said. She smiled. "You won't ever have to beg."

The boil got bigger and became very tender. I couldn't swallow without pain. A few days later, Ma took the hand-held mirror and let me see that the boil had developed a whitehead.

"It's time," my mother said and grabbed her sewing kit and took out a large needle.

"Let me see," my brother said. "Let me hold the mirror."

My mother was rummaging through her cooking ware, turning over pots and pans.

"What happened to my matches?" she asked. She kept searching until she found a few matches and then she struck one on the cement and heated the needle in the flame till it glowed red.

Ma leaned closer to me. I saw her hands moving toward my throat. Imagining the painful stab of the hot needle, I jerked and screamed. Then I felt the sharp pain and my mother's fingers squeezing the boil. I clenched my teeth and looked in the mirror. The pus erupted from the boil and ran down my neck, and then blood poured out along with a clear fluid.

"Yuck," my brother said.

After a few days, the boil completely disappeared. I was no longer afraid of becoming a beggar, but my brother and I never thought about stealing the beggar's coins again. The next time we went out to the streets, we steered clear of his corner. There were soldiers working on the broken engine of a deuce-and-a-half truck. Its hood was propped up, and its engine parts were spread out on rags that lay on the oil-stained dirt. I ran to take a look at the truck and get some candy. I hoped that someday one of the soldiers would recognize me and pick me up and take me to America. But the soldiers only wiped their oil-and-grease-covered hands, gave us candy and gum, and then turned back to the truck.

We went out to the streets to escape our mother's anger. Walking along the walls of residences, we peeked through the windows of neighbors' houses and through the screen doors of bars where soldiers played pool. We looked up from the streets into hotel windows and watched the ceiling fans and the shadows of the blades spinning slowly. Sometimes we could see the shadow of a man or woman. We played King of the Coke Bottle Caps with other children and spent afternoons knocking over stacks of caps in the shadows of the prison walls across the street. The streets were always busy with traffic: mopeds, bicycles, pedestrians, and, in the mornings and late afternoons, water buffalo.

We collected old cloth name tags, even though we couldn't read the names. We dug up live rounds from the dirt on the street after they had been run over by cars and trucks. Sometimes the rains of the wet season washed the dirt off the rounds and exposed their shiny brass shells. Eventually, we learned which kind of weapon each round belonged to: pistol or rifle or heavy machine gun. The rounds contained gunpowder, so they never stayed intact for very long. We unscrewed the bullets and tapped the black powder onto gum wrappers and set the wrappers on fire with matches; then we watched the powder burst into flames.

When we grew tired from the heat and all our running on the dusty streets, we went home and sat with our mother on the floor mats and asked her to tell us about our fathers.

"Are they still alive?" we asked. "Are they really dead?"

"Dung, your father died while crossing a bridge, and Sa's father died in a helicopter accident."

"But you said my father was shot," I said. "And Sa's father hanged."

"What's true is what I tell you," she said, scowling. She grew tired of our questions, so one day she brought home a small transistor radio. Then she turned it on for us so that we could listen to the news of the war for ourselves.

My brother and I sat on the floor mats and listened to the voice coming from the radio tell us about the weather. We listened to the voice report the battles. We stayed in the bungalow and sat still as the voice told us the stories of soldiers killed in the war. Once, the voice cackled and wheezed and told the story of a soldier who was shot while dragging the body of his buddy across a bridge.

"Is that the bridge my father crossed?" I asked my mother.

"Was there a name for the bridge?" She hadn't been listening to the radio and was fanning herself to keep cool in the midday heat.

"The voice didn't say," I said.

"It could be the bridge," she said. "He died on a narrow, wooden bridge. It didn't have a name."

I wondered if my father thought about my mother before he was killed in the war between the North and the South. But I also imagined that he jumped off the bridge and dove into the river water. I imagined that enemy soldiers fired shots once they had him in their sights. I saw him swimming underwater while bullets ripped the surface. I fantasized that he swam downriver along the banks and under the bramble of deadfall and branches, then escaped and ran toward our bungalow into my mother's arms.

I wondered if my father ever knew about me. While I sat and listened to the stories coming over the radio, I wondered if the voice on the radio knew my father. I wanted to find the radio's voice. I wondered where the voice came from and how the radio worked. I wanted to ask it questions. It seemed to know more about the war than my mother did, so I thought that maybe it knew something about my father. After a while, I asked my mother where the voice came from.

"It comes through the antenna," she said.

So I ran out to the streets in search of antennae and found them sticking out of armored personnel carriers and tanks and protruding from jeeps and trucks. I asked the Vietnamese soldiers who sat next to the Americans about the voice. They looked at me and then spoke to the Americans in their language, and all the soldiers laughed.

Sometimes, when our mother wasn't looking or she was gone, my brother and I banged the radio on the cement floor. We turned the knobs and dials, but there was always the voice or the crackle of static. We even took the radio apart and inspected the transistors and copper wiring, but we always managed to put it back together before our mother came home.

The radio just seemed to be a black box that hacked and wheezed out reports about someone's brother or father. It spoke to us in the morning and at night, reading off lists of names. It recited the names in the morning while our mother cooked us breakfast, in the afternoon while we took our naps, and in the evening when we crawled into the mosquito netting strung up over our sleeping mats on the patio. We didn't comprehend the meaning of those lists. We didn't realize those names would never be announced again.

The storms ended. The flood waters receded from our alley, and the men in the green uniforms returned to the doorsteps of our bungalow. They strolled down our alley dressed in fatigues, wearing web belts and shoulder harnesses and holstered pistols. They jumped off the backs of deuce-and-a-halfs in the various greens of their camouflage, in drab olive-green fatigues with deep pockets, and in worn-out mechanic's greens mired with oil and dirt from repairing the engines of tanks or working under the bellies of Hueys and Chinooks. They knocked on our door in the amber green of shirts and trousers burned by the hot steam of the ironing press. They stepped out of jeeps in the emerald green of dress uniforms worn for traveling or staying in the garrison. Sometimes they approached our bungalow with smiles, but most often with stern looks and tired eyes.

They were the men in the green uniforms, the men who threw us gum and patted our shoulders and brought us toys. But when they came to see our mother, they slipped off their black boots and their pressed uniforms. When they left, their uniforms were creased and crumpled. Sometimes my brother and I spied on our mother and her clients through the cracks in the bamboo partition. As the clients undressed, we saw them change from green to the color of the chameleons that we caught on rocks as they changed from emerald to stone.

On one of those days soon after the storms had passed, when the cement blocks of our bungalow were still wet, my brother and I walked to the neighborhood's rain gutters and I showered under the run-off. With our clothes wet, our hair matted down, and our rubber sandals squeaking, we started down the alley towards home. The tomato vines had been stripped of their leaves, and all the fruit was crushed and scattered across the muddy ground. The bushes of chili peppers and grapefruit trees were usually shaded. Now, with the broad leaves of the banana trees ripped to shreds, they sat exposed to the hot sun.

As we approached the patio, we saw that a soldier was stretched out in our hammock. His field cap covered his face. One arm rested on his stomach and the other hung off the side of the hammock. The fingers of one hand gripped the blue plastic straps of a pair of roller skates. The metal skates shone in the sunlight. I looked at Sa, and I knew that we wondered the same thing: maybe this soldier was one of our fathers. As we stepped closer, our sandals squeaked. We stood beside the hammock and looked down at the soldier. He seemed to be asleep. The bungalow door was open. I knew our mother was inside and would come out at any moment. The soldier had a dark tan and curly black hair. Suddenly, he kicked up his feet, sat up, and grabbed my brother in one swift movement. He smiled and laughed—his laughter infectious. He picked up the roller skates and pointed toward my brother's bare feet. Smiling, my brother took off his sandals, and the soldier strapped on the skates for him. Then he gripped Sa's arms and pushed him backward on the cement patio. I laughed. The soldier let him go. Sa stood stiffly with his arms out and his knees locked straight, then kicked his legs and rolled until he tumbled onto the cement.

My mother came out of the bungalow and handed the soldier a glass of lemonade. With ice in it, the glass was sweating in the heat of the afternoon. My mother must have gotten the ice from the market. It was rare that she bought blocks of ice, which were wrapped in burlap bags and stored in sawdust. But once in a while she bought it when she crushed green tea leaves and made iced-tea, and among her utensils was an awl that she used for chipping it. I looked at the soldier and at the chips floating in the glass. I thought he was one of our fathers because he was special enough to get ice in his glass.

"Can I have some ice?" I asked. I knew there was a whole block somewhere in the bungalow.

"Me, too!" said my brother, who slipped on the roller skates and nearly fell face first on the cement patio.

Our mother went into the bungalow. We heard her chipping the block, heard each strike of the awl. The soldier pushed my brother around some more. Sa rolled back and forth on the patio and bounced from wall to wall.

When the chipping sound stopped, our mother appeared at the door with two chunks of ice and gave them to us. The chunk was so cold in my hand that I kept switching it from one palm to the other. I bit off a small piece, and the ice was so cold on my teeth that they hurt.

The soldier drank from his glass of lemonade. My brother rolled around clumsily on the patio and fell again, bumping into the soldier's legs. As the soldier tried to haul my brother onto his feet, some of the lemonade spilled from his glass and left a wet spot on his trousers.

My mother put her hands on my shoulders. She patted me on the head and looked into my eyes.

"Take Sa down the street to the sidewalk," she said, "and practice riding the skates." She gave me some money. "You can buy a drink from the vendors when you're both thirsty."

My brother held on to my arm to keep himself steady as he stepped off the patio, and I pushed and pulled him down the alley and out into the street. I looked back down the tunnel of the alley, toward the patio and the hammock. My mother and the soldier had disappeared into the bungalow.

It didn't take us long to learn how to roll around on the skates without falling down. We took turns skating and chasing each other on the sidewalk and the hard-packed dirt of the street. It was so hot that we skated only in the shaded sections of the sidewalk. The streets were quiet while everyone took an afternoon nap, so we skated back and forth down the whole length of the sidewalk. We started out slowly and then we skated faster. The ball bearings in the wheels hissed. We kicked our feet behind us and pushed ourselves forward and felt the wind of speed against our cheeks.

We skated until we were thirsty and then we went to the vendors. We stood by as the vendor crushed sugarcane for our drinks by drawing the stalks through two wooden rollers. While we waited, he cut off two small slices and gave them to us to chew on.

When we were tired from the sun and the skating, we headed back to the alley. The door to the bungalow was shut. I had on the skates and stepped up onto the patio and skated to the door. I tried to open it, pulling and yanking on the doorknob, but it was locked. I heard my mother's voice whispering inside. I pounded on the door with my fists.

"Let us in!" I said. "We're home."

No one answered. No one came to the door. I pounded harder, and as I slammed my fist again, the skates kicked out from under me. I stuck my arm out straight to cushion my fall. When my hand hit the wet cement, a sharp pain shot up from my elbow. I screamed. My brother pounded on the door, shouting, "Come out! Dung broke his arm!"

The door opened, and my mother came out. She was pulling her shirt over her pants, and she looked down at me while I cradled the injured elbow with my other arm.

"What did you do?" she said. Her client stood behind her.

The pain in my elbow hurt so much that I could barely speak. I swallowed a big gulp of air. I tried not to cry in front of the soldier.

"He slipped and fell on his arm," Sa said. "I think he broke it."

My mother got down on her knees and squeezed my elbow. "Does that hurt?"

"It hurts," I said, almost in a whisper.

She tried to straighten my elbow. I screamed. The soldier knelt beside me. He pressed his fingers into my tender elbow. I winced and screamed again. Then he probed my bony arm, touching gently. When he finished, he looked up at my mother and shook his head.

"Your arm isn't broken," she said. "You just jammed it really good."

The soldier said something to my mother and then walked quickly out to the alley. When he came back, he held some blue cloth in his hands.

"He's going to put your elbow in a sling," my mother said. She saw the fear in my eyes.

The soldier lifted my injured arm, wrapped the blue cloth under my elbow, and tied the sling around my neck. He smiled, and his brown eyes were bright in the afternoon sun. He said a few things to my mother, disappeared into the bungalow, and came back out. I knew he was about to leave, but when he turned to say goodbye, he brought his arms from behind his back and gave me a tea box sealed with green tape.

"There's a gift for you inside," my mother said. "But you can't open the box until your elbow heals."

I waited for a week. My elbow still hurt a little, but my mother said I could open the box. I took a knife and cut the tape and pulled out something with green bands and moving dials.

"A watch!" I said.

"Now you can tell time," my mother said as she stitched a patch over a hole on my brother's shorts.

"How can I do that?" I asked.

"I'll show you," she said. "See the little hands?"

"What hands?"

She pointed to the face of the watch. "These little things. They're called hands."

"They don't look like hands," I said. "They look like needles."

"OK, then. The little needle shows the hours. The big needle shows the minutes."

"What are hours and minutes?" I asked.

"Ways to tell the time," she said. "Days are made of hours, and hours are made of minutes."

"How many hours in a minute?" I asked.

"Minutes are smaller," she said, laughing. "Hours are made of minutes."

"Then why is the big needle the minutes? Shouldn't the big needle be the hours?"

"Because minutes happen faster," she said, exasperated, and continued her stitching.

I didn't understand the concept of time. I only knew the passing of days and nights between my mother's leaving and her eventual return. I knew the moments between the arrival and departure of my mother's clients, when they entered and left our alley.

We never knew where our mother's clients came from. My brother and I knew only that the land and the air and the sea brought them. We watched them as they lumbered under the weight of their war gear and marched down the loading ramps of cargo planes and rode into town on trucks and jeeps.

We cheered them as they disembarked from the decks of warships and landed on our coast with their rifles and steel pots and field caps shielding their eyes. We watched them as they jumped from the bellies of helicopters hovering over the landing zones and then flattening the marsh grass into a carpet. We spied on them while we crouched behind the grassy berms bordering the landing zones. We watched them loading crates of weapons and boxes of ammo and medical supplies into the backs of deuce-and-a-halfs.

On many afternoons, we stood outside the gates of the prison or the army base on the other side of town and studied the soldiers, their uniforms and equipment. In a game that we played, we categorized them into the foot soldiers and the sailors, the men who drove tanks, the pilots who flew jets and helicopters. Then there were the soldiers our fathers must have known: the ones who patrolled the jungles and never came back. We spotted the soldiers who worked as cooks in the mess halls, and the soldiers who guarded the prisons, and the ones who worked in the Quonset huts and never got killed.

I knew time as the moments my brother and I roamed the streets and harbors and watched the men of war—the men who sometimes strolled down our alley. Time was when we peeked through the cracks in the bamboo partition at our mother and her clients. Time was the number of waterdrops plunking into the cistern. That was all I knew of seconds, minutes, and hours.

And though I didn't know how to read the moving hands, I knew that it was a gift, that the watch was mine.

The dry season brought long, hot days and dusty streets, and the grass in the alley became brittle. Sometimes in the days and nights, I could hear the dry blades rustle and break under the heavy combat boots of my mother's clients. I heard the grasshoppers pop out of the brittle grass whenever someone entered the alley.

Sometimes when my brother and I were supposed to be napping, we watched the black wasps crawl in and out of a clay nest above the doorway of our bungalow. In the evenings we slapped away the mosquitoes probing the netting pitched over our mats. We tested out our homemade firecrackers by sticking them into anthills and lighting them and watching them explode. We stuck firecrackers into the mouths of frogs and blew them up. We chased after lizards with long bodies and tails that rasped against the cement walls of our bungalow. Sometimes we caught a praying mantis and put it into a jar with a black wasp we had knocked down from its nest with the broom. There were more insects in the dry season—more grasshoppers and cicadas, dragonflies and houseflies—buzzing loudly and crawling on our bodies. Sometimes while we ate on the floor, shiny gold beetles flew into our bungalow and landed at our feet. My mother told us it was good luck if they flew into a home. One day while we ate our favorite meal of pork and rice, a gold beetle landed on the cement floor right next to my mother's Sterno. I caught it and held it in my hands. I could almost see my face reflected in the gold wings. I wished that someday my brother and mother and I could go to America, and then I tossed the gold beetle into the air and watched the blur of its wings as it flew away.

from *A Year without Sleep* _____

To Wish to Go Home

Luis Garcia, rosaries and tears tattooed around his wrists and down his fingers, was first to swing and wasn't stopped. The blue spider-webbing on his upper arm was sprayed red as his fists came down on Muldoon, whose nose disappeared in splat and tooth crunch, lips flapping, face greased with blood. Then there was a hollow cracking of ribs.

Everyone watched in silence. Muldoon had gotten his wish. He'd been asking everyone to break his bones or shoot him somewhere safe, somewhere the damage would get him home, just home, ever talking about his family, telling stories like how he gave his thirty-year-old uncle mumps and made him sterile, for which he was hated by his aunt, or rattling names off of all his cousins and their favorite foods and movies—having memorized it all and being related to half of Ireland—a Catholic who knew how to pop Garcia's fuse by insulting the Virgin.

When he stopped, Garcia threw the sack of Muldoon in a jeep to drive him to the aid station. On the way, they hit a mine. Muldoon flew from the jeep and was impaled on a broken tree. Luis Garcia's hands, their blue tattoos and bloody knuckles, were blown from his arms and fell to the road, then were dropped in a rubber sack to ship home.

Soon, his hands would wiggle in the earth. Opening, closing against the weight of a soldier's field. Everybody wants to go home. Everybody always wants to. In Luis's mother's house there will be a *nicho* altar with his name spelled in tiny nuts and seeds, a plaster statue of Virgin Mary, rosary, a bleeding tin heart with a crucifix he brought her from a trip, his Purple Heart, his photo in a uniform, his Spanish Bible, his high-school diploma earned at night after working all day in a gas station, a bottle of the Mexican beer he drank on the stoop hot summers when his blood was sweating, a pile of letters in a ribbon, and a diamond engagement ring in a little box marked "María, *mi corazón*" that will be found at the bottom of his duffel bag.

Muldoon's house will be hushed the first night. No one will believe it. Everyone will think it was a mistake. They will discuss it in those terms, drink a few beers and cups of tea, waiting for the real news. They will stare at Muldoon's face in his box and still not believe it. Long years of trying to believe it will begin.

There will be great wailing under two roofs, black storms of talk and silence, suspicions of betrayal casting shadows across the light of many faces. Bitter words will hiss, new worlds begin, dark collaborations be discussed, clothing and property dispersed, and two young women will sit, and sit. Their hearts and brains will be numb like stone. They will watch their dreams migrate then disappear, and will die a thousand times while the men who sent their lives away sit at a polished table in Paris discussing fine art and wine.

Coming Upon a Massacre

After the Americans disappeared, he came out from the tree line surrounding the clearing of the small village and crouched, looking around. Then, with both knees grinding in earth, his mouth dropped open and he couldn't shut it.

The shock didn't last. He'd seen such things before, and spent those nights chewing manioc and rice, stoned on wild marijuana, sometimes discussing the nature of war with his comrades, the invasions that cause them, the things men do, but usually they gambled and talked about women.

It worried him the shock didn't last. It didn't always worry him, but this time he noticed. The moon had a red streak, and looked like a skull floating on a black river. It was a long time before he realized it was the marijuana working. It felt like hours before he realized, then days. Maybe he sat there a year, or two. Perhaps three.

Watching a delicate insect crawl over water beads on a leaf in the moonlight, he was calmed by the thought that he would wake up soon, then seized by the terror of knowing he already had.

In the Orphanage

Rain drizzled on the panes while they wondered if a spider's legs grow out of its head, and if, when they banged their bread on the table, it would bend.

Who are those people driving up, they thought, are they for me, will they mind if my feet get wet going out, and what happens to a bird in the rain anyway, how can it fly in water?

They think the soldiers are working hard, and twist little dolls for them from wrapping paper and straw so they'll have someone to admire.

They came from the shelters after the bombing and it started to rain, so they went to the windows and watched the pontoon bridges pull from their anchors and drift, believing all roads leading back to the world are meant to float away.

On the Way to Work in the Fire Zone

Leaves shudder as trucks and jeeps roll by, then shudder again when something explodes.

Chin on chest, she stares down. Her husband's eyes flicker with the light of a car on fire, reflections on convex shields, flames on the frozen blind. He melts over the curb.

Birds never seen in the city before have come to roost there in flocks. They blanket the overturned stalls.

She screams and yanks her husband by the belt, still arguing, hysterical now, over which of them checked the windows and back door locks before they left home.

The Last Bear

When the last cover of leaves dropped in defoliant, the young soldiers who had been feeding the only bear left in the zoo could no longer cross the sniper yard. For months they had smuggled food across the darkness—apples, bread, canned chili, stew, and candy—and the bear also ate its mate, as had all the other now dead animals in the zoo. It would never be safe again to go over there, so they watched him die after lapping up an exploded can of beer they managed to toss across the wire.

Afterwards, they all talked about what happens when a way of life becomes impossible. And then about what government is, realizing it is not a thing they could ever understand in twenty lifetimes. They sat looking through field glasses at the bear floating like an island swarmed with flies on its concrete platform, feeling like the animals of a zoo as large as life itself, animals transported worlds away from their own habitats, subsisting on strange words and food that would only weaken and kill them.

Another World We Missed

In first light it was all coming down, stars and uterine nebulae, a wax moon, jets, bombs and rockets, hot ash sparks drifting on thick blood air, and we were thinking how clear the meaning of vanity is in a context of stars and in the light of our sun which one day must consume itself and all we think is important.

Looking back to Earth, we saw the buttress roots of a tropical grove in motion, undulating veins, as if the bark was crawling and the trees would leap, but moving closer saw they were swarmed with ants bearing tiny human skulls and bones, furniture, house trailers, tools and cars and games.

They found another world we missed.

If they looked up at us in the rising light, our eyes would have seemed like planets, our teeth dull streaks across the sky, our curiosity and fear a negligible motion.

But they did not pause or notice. Their paths were shimmering fibers that streamed two ways: one with the weightless load of desire, the other with results. And though both plunge into darkness in the end—one to Earth, the other through the beak of a fallen bird—they know, as we can never, what they must do to get home.

Three Poems

WOULD THAT

Would that emptiness
could be tied down to paper
Would that the unfathomable
could write in a straight line
Would that the river of stars
could fly through the lines of little words
hold all the sorrows of our passing lives.

THE PERIOD

Yellow leaves tumble
a comma
to return to each season,

Each strain of white hair
an exclamation mark
never to return.

Willingly or not, our life moves toward a point of infinity
until it falls
a period.

FIN DE SIÈCLE

keep a few lines of poem
to exist in my place
this century does not need to remain
for next century to read it as a passing sign.

Translations by Kevin Bowen and Nguyen Ba Chung

Four Poems

TRIVIAL DETAILS

Inside an old car a heart sat behind the wheel
To circulate along the blood avenues
Where battles and a chaotic retreat occurred
In which my father was killed

I grazed her breasts and was wondering why she did not smile
It was what I had waited for all night inside a hut lit by a lantern
Her teeth resembled the keyboard of an unplugged organ

As a carpenter Christ should have made himself a coffin beforehand
Maybe that's only a trivial detail
But we live in a practical world, and trivial details are often what
    generate beliefs

How to jump from the stove to the pan and back without tripping
My face is a doorknob
If you turn and enter, behind it is a void I have to stock with things
    to convert into a warehouse before sudden dusk

Wolves are sharing the corpse of a crow and hurling blood at the sky
There are fixed values and unnecessary rituals carried out
    because of instinctual fear

"Ah, in the end He has come," the secretary says, bowing to the God
    of miserable fates,
Then throws his ink pen at the goldfish inside the glass tank
That tiny world soon has the color of the sea
By doing so he becomes a creator

I watch a film with a telescope and imagine that I am someone
    from another planet
Who abandoned his own kind a long time ago

A fat man kneels next to a woman who has just died
Says to take some of my flesh with you
Which you will need, when your own flesh has rotted
That is a dream I often have in my evening sleep

When bored and feeling rich I will travel
To a country where everything is coincidental
Man is born to be satisfied with waiting
Where I was born to wait for myself

The door slams with the vague sound of a collision from the other
    bank of the river where fishermen are tapping their boats to chase
    fish into nets.

INSIDE SUBMARINES

We live inside odd-shaped submarines
chasing after secrets and the darkness of the ocean
on a voyage toward plastic horizons
where vague connections are always out of reach
and hopes are not deployed
before the storm arrives and the alarm command starts
to rouse the last illusions to stand up and put life jackets on
looking to each other for help

Once I was at the equator
trying to slice the Earth in half along the dotted line
but someone held my hand and said:
"If you do that, friend, water will fall into the void,
and then our submarine
won't have any place to dive."

AUTUMN SONG

Like an inverted hat in sunlight and the uselessness
   of a misplaced article
I realize I don't even resemble myself in old photographs
In newer photographs I am a color reproduction
   of an outdoor concert without listeners
Next to kinsmen of a different faith
That was a cloudy day and the faces were lit by flashlight
I walked slowly away from the looks

Autumn is like an old immigrant in old clothes
Forlorn and complaining about changes
I am not garrulous, it's just that I can't keep a secret
The hopelessness of unions makes me want to hear
Sounds of leaves falling on the chest
Of a man lying under a tree
With a hand grenade inside his pants pocket

Bread made of buckwheat mixed with some garlic
I don't like tossing food to pigeons in a plaza
They do nothing but peck and copulate
How did aristocrats make love in the past—like pigeons?
Books describe most of them as degenerates
Did they pluck feathers from birds and point at the moon?
If they raped they had to waste a lot of time undressing
People say that my country has been constantly raped!

As a child I spat into the palm of a blind beggar
What should I do now in autumn?

IN THE SILICON VALLEY

There are climates that can wear out shoes like acid
The view out the window is always cut by rain and sunlight,
    and fuzzy calculations on a computer
I live in a valley where people will saw off their own leg to sell
    to buy a house
All the sublimeness of language has died in a jar breeding
    an artificial fetus
There are many such artificial children in the Silicon Valley.
    They wear plastic name tags and colorful ties

It's not at all difficult to create an impression
Mix arsenic with wine to drink with dragon meat. Look at the sky
while stuffing a hand into your pants pocket to find a morsel of
bread without breaking it. Lick your own sole then stand straight up
to greet a crowd attending a funeral. In the end everything needs to
happen exactly according to the daily schedule

Thule is a remote settlement in the northwest of Greenland
    only 450 miles from the top of the world
I want to go there and attempt a journey on dogsled
In this valley even flies can't conceive
Within ten years all the mountains in this place will be
    upside-down triangles
The moon will be pulled to Earth by a giant cable
This peninsula will be pushed out to sea by an earthquake
    then reattached with Super Glue

At night a train passes ringing a bell, and a barrier is lowered
These are the last sounds of a day in a heaven made of plastic
Before dejection melts with the burning smell of a car collision.

Translations by Linh Dinh

Two Poems

AT THE BARBERSHOP

Me, if I look into the barbershop mirror I want to be a revolutionary   it's not clear, between hairstyles and the art of cleaning out ear wax, which is a more satisfying revolution. I am a dark-skinned, working-class man, and don't normally pay attention to that value, but if someone pastes the color red or white on my eyes, I go crazy immediately   my entire body darkens to the color of blood pudding mixed with the aroma of mint leaves and peanuts. I hate to join the uprising of those at the wine bar but each evening I'm drowned in that piss smell. I crave the sort of wine brewed from the sea   the sea speaks a universal language   the sea cuts hair and cleans out ear wax several times a month   each clump of hair each clump of ear wax   is a ship carrying consciousness of democracy to help shriveled old men become boys with large foreheads incubating dreams of becoming the president.

CHICKEN-FEATHER-DUCK-FEATHER SKY

Chicken-feather-duck-feather sky   a sneeze redolent of five spices. Schools over flames, one and all can learn about fear, the lessons dragging from one night to the next each night fear is honed into a sword planted on a head   a place where the wind howls. Fear! That's the kind of music I want to hear   not always good but a safe kind of music. I listen to it endlessly   I listen until death and the criminal just want to return the corpses.

Translations by Linh Dinh

The Self-Portrait

I am a painter, not a writer. I wish to make this point clear from the start—not as a plea for generosity from the reader, but to remind myself that I write this story for my own sake and for the sake of the painting I have just completed. The second thing I will mention is that the story is written for one other person. However, no matter whom it is written for—whether for you, the reader, or this other person, who is, in fact, a barber—what I write will still be a kind of confession.

I cannot honestly remember how many months have passed since the day I first walked into the barbershop and recognized him. Since then, however, I've forced myself to pedal the two or three kilometers once a month to have him cut my hair. I have no idea how long ago it was that I started slaving over this oil painting either. Oil was unfamiliar to me until then, but I knew I could not treat this subject with watercolors or lacquers. Neither the quick brushstrokes of watercolor nor the dazzling illusory atmospherics of lacquer can satisfy the demands of an artist who wishes to build an understanding of himself and judge himself by his strokes. Only this morning did I finish the painting. Now I sit in front of the self-portrait and face myself. How can I describe it? Dear reader, imagine the face of a man sitting as if nailed down to a barber's chair. A broad, white cloth covers his chest; a very large human face nearly fills the whole canvas. Beams of light pour down on a head and illuminate it as if they were thousands of candles. Half of the head is covered with thick, bushy hair and looks like a mysterious dark forest. The other half, already clipped, looks at first glimpse very much like a human brain. Around it, the skin is peeled back, the flesh exposed, as if left open after an operation. As for the face of the man, the customer, his two eyes stare up at the source of the beams, questioning, filled with anxiety. The lower part of his face seems to be hidden beneath a mask: the chin, the corners of the mouth are completely concealed by soap bubbles. The mouth cannot be seen clearly except as a black dime floating on the foam.

At first glance, the face seems extremely ugly and strange, but the more I look at it, the more it resembles mine. *It is my own face, my inner face,* I say to myself. It is the face I wore when I rested my head on the back of the wooden chair and looked up at the face of the barber.

To follow the story, friend, you must know that about eight years ago I worked on a remote battlefield along the southwestern border. I was ordered at that time to return north to take part in an overseas art exhibition with other Ha Noi artists. The paintings and sketches I had made were numerous; they filled an entire shelter in our base camp located in the heart of the forest. I was allowed to select one-third of them. To transport even this fraction meant that the chief at each liaison post I passed had to assign one of his soldiers to help me carry the paintings.

On the journey, we had to cross a border area that was filled with enemy special forces. Food was scarce, and the area was well known as a breeding ground for malaria. We stopped for a day of rest before passing through it to get to a shelter on the hill above the liaison post. It was noon, and I was idly sketching the stones and trees in front of the shelter when a soldier with a pale complexion and bluish lips climbed up the steep slope, walked straight to where I was sitting, and sat down to watch me draw. We got into a conversation, and after a while the soldier began to beg me to draw his portrait.

I felt offended. I was a painter, not a commercial portraitist! I gave him a cold stare. He looked hurt. He studied the stern look on my face for a while, then turned his back and silently walked down the slope.

When we set off the next morning, I was surprised to find that the soldier who had asked for the sketch was the one assigned to carry my paintings on the next leg of the journey. This fact troubled me; it was not a comfortable situation.

When we left the liaison post, our guide informed us that we would have to move quickly when we reached the spot where the path sloped down to a brook that opened to clearings on both sides. Other groups had been attacked by rangers there, or detected by scout planes passing overhead. For the most part, traveling through forests is much the same—crossing passes, hills, brooks—but in reality, no place is like another. It was afternoon when we began climbing up a gently sloping mountain. The sides of the path were covered with reeds in full blossom, and the scene was picturesque. Tall, pointed rocks called cat's ear stones were all around. When we reached the other side of the mountain, the reeds grew thickly and the ground was black with stones. We climbed down, gasping for air, our fingers gripping each stone top as we struggled down.

At the base of the mountain, the stream ran through the clearing. The stony bank must have been about five hundred meters long. The brook grew wider, splashing and roaring over a bed of knife-sharp stones. Even with an entire day's rest, I was exhausted after crossing the mountain. With great difficulty, I made my way carefully to the middle of the rapids. Then I grew nervous, finding myself gradually falling behind. Suddenly, my foot slipped and got stuck in an underwater crevice. I lost my balance and threw my arms in the air, gesturing wildly.

Although he was far ahead, the soldier carrying my paintings saw me and hurried back. Had he not reached me in time, I would have been swept underwater. He took the rucksack from my back and hung it on top of his chest, then raised me up and helped me pull my foot out. As we walked on, he held me by the arm. I gasped for breath, my body covered in sweat from the effort, and my vision suddenly blurred. I seemed to see a thousand fire-flies dancing about me.

"Comrade, try harder." The soldier encouraged me as he walked by my side. "I'll help you walk faster, then we'll take a rest on the other side. If a scout plane comes, we can sit down there and it won't see us."

I couldn't keep up with the others anymore. On the other side of the brook, the soldier massaged my feet with tiger balm. From this point on, there were only the two of us. We traveled alone through the forest. I couldn't hold anything, so the soldier had to carry the rucksack with my paintings, which was twice as heavy as that of an ordinary traveler, on his back, and my own rucksack on his chest. The load must have totaled sixty to seventy kilos, and the soldier didn't seem strong enough to carry it all.

Although I have not mentioned it, you may imagine how chastened I felt when the soldier lifted up my paintings. It was no longer just my belong-ings, but also myself that he was burdened with on this journey. Up until this point I had always considered myself a sensible person, someone with a fair amount of self-esteem. I would have thought it fair if the soldier had been indifferent or left me behind to hobble through the forest on my own. I had always believed that people got what they gave. The soldier's behavior had to be attributed to a kind of generosity. Generosity? I was his superior! An established painter! Up to that point, I had only known the generosity exercised by a superior toward his inferior. And now I was being treated generously by an inferior!

Unable to reach the liaison station, we had to spend the night in the for-est. The soldier fixed my hammock for me, then sat beside me on a rock, cradling his weapon while keeping guard. How could I sleep? I got up and sat next to him on the rock. The forest was dark and menacing at night.

"Comrade, I'm sorry about yesterday," I whispered. "Tomorrow I'll draw you a portrait—a good one."

"If only a photographer was here, I wouldn't have bothered you!" He said slowly, "Unfortunately, there aren't any in the forest."

He paused for a while and then continued. "Recently, I met a new recruit from the North and learned from him that my family had been told that I was killed. From here it takes a year for a letter to reach the North. I've wanted to send home a picture—something that my mother has long desired. But it's impossible to have a picture taken."

I interrupted him. "So I'll draw a lifelike portrait of you, and I'll personally deliver the picture and a letter to your family."

In my enthusiasm, I suggested finding some wood to make a fire so that I could start right away, but he dissuaded me. "Don't make a fire," he said.

The next morning he led me to the new post.

I did the portrait in half an hour, unable to spend any more time on it. I had to join my group for the next leg of their journey, and the soldier had to make preparations to carry the gear of some high-ranking cadre to another post. He didn't even have time to write a letter, and was only able to jot down his address. So we parted.

Success in art is sometimes a matter of luck, and only artists may fully understand this. You must find it strange—or maybe not—that this hastily drawn portrait of the soldier became my masterpiece, famous not only in our country but overseas as well. I could never have foreseen this turn of events. The miserable thing was that all those pictures and sketches that I had taken such pains to transport from the battlefield did not have a very long life, although most of them were displayed and reproduced now and then in magazines and newspapers. The sketch done by the "commercial portraitist," however, lived on as the landmark of my career during the years of the war.

It was just luck that brought me across the threshold of that barbershop. It was a lackluster place in the northwestern part of the city, located on a narrow side road where I had never before set foot. My home and office were situated at the other end of the city. It was a summer morning; I had gone to an office in that part of the city, but had missed the person I was supposed to meet. I rode my bicycle around the neighborhood, admiring the curving lines of the roofs and walls of that ancient section of the city. For a few hours, I explored things from a painter's point of view. If I had been carrying a pencil and paper in my pocket that morning, I would never have come up with the idea of getting my hair cut. I walked into a barbershop, but both chairs were occupied. I walked out and pushed my bicycle beside a long, narrow wall. At the end of the wall, near an alley, was a stall that served food and drinks. A large group of young people was sitting there, leisurely sipping tea and smoking. Next to the stall was another barbershop, but this did not look very much like a shop at all. It was just a nylon army poncho slung over a small patch of earth littered with the remnants of customers' hair. At the center stood an old wooden chair that looked like it had been constructed by the barber himself; across its back lay a fairly clean white cloth. The barber was not there, only an old woman sweeping the remaining locks of hair into a corner. I leaned the bicycle against the wall and stepped in. At first glance, the shop did not appear at all inviting, but then I saw on the wall, above the mirror, a reproduction of my celebrated picture: the sketch of the soldier who had carried my paintings eight years before. Its presence gave me a good feeling about the place.

Only when the old woman looked up did I realize that she was blind. She must have heard my footsteps. With the broomstick in her hands, she slowly raised her dimmed eyes toward me; I noticed brightness and delight gradually spread over her face.

"Will you sit down and wait for a few minutes? My son will soon finish his tea and take care of you right away. Will you wait—it will only be for a few minutes."

"Yes, that's fine," I said and sat down in the chair. The old woman resumed sweeping. Perhaps fearing that I would go away, she raised her head again and said, "The newspaper is on the table. Would you like to read it?"

I reached for the paper sitting among rows of bottles and began reading page four, which covered world events.

There was quite a bit of news. I'm not crazy about soccer, but the report of a match in a capital city in Latin America was so engrossing that I did not notice when the barber returned. I remained absorbed in the article while he draped a white cloth across my chest, straightened my hair, and tested his clippers. I think he might have made some comment about my hair being so bushy and my needing a cut badly. It was not until he held my head straight and then tilted it up a little that I lowered the newspaper.

"Do you want it cut in the same style?" he asked.

"Yes, please."

The barber was in his thirties. He had a face that I thought I had seen before and the pale complexion of someone who lived in the forest. He was wearing a faded white cotton shirt and a pair of old, patched army trousers, which had the perfumed scent typical of barber's clothing.

As was my habit, I chatted. "You must have few customers coming down this alley."

"Not many, but enough. Most are regulars. Lately business is not so good."

"Not good for some businesses, but good for others—like black-marketing maybe. As for your business, people's hair always grows and always needs cutting."

"Yes, but only when people have spare money will they think about their appearance: their teeth, their hair . . ."

"Well, I give in. How long have you been doing this?"

"For nearly fifteen years. Since I was at school, and before that I was in the army."

I have a bad habit of forgetting things I should remember, but as compensation, I am gifted with a memory that allows me, in a flash, to see each and every detail of a particular day of my life. I experience moments when I was six as clearly as looking at an old photo. I finally recognized the barber.

How I wished that I could have put a mask on or shrunk to the size of a pea in that chair! What can I say to make you understand the feeling of guilt that overcame me? Have you ever moved house? When you have to move, you suddenly find deep in a drawer or underneath a bed something you thought you had lost a long time ago, something you were unable to find after looking everywhere. Some are small, insignificant things; others call up a pleasant memory; and still others arouse nasty memories of incidents you had thought long forgotten. That inanimate, insensible object discovered in a dark, dirty corner slowly crawls out, whispers to you, criticizes, accuses you.

Why didn't I take the portrait to your family? Why didn't I keep my promise? I remembered promising you and myself with great conviction, forcefulness, and sincerity. That night, sitting next to you on the rock in the deep forest by the border, I was determined to personally deliver the portrait to your family, even if it meant going through a storm of enemy bullets or leaping through fire. It seemed a small return for the unspoken but immense generosity you had shown me. At that time, tears rose in my eyes when you said that your mother had been misinformed—told that you were dead. The next morning when we parted, I repeated my promise over and over. I remember holding your hand as if I could not let you go. I hugged you. How deceitful I was, though, deceiving even myself when I kissed you before setting off on the next leg of my journey.

I traveled on foot for three months before reaching Ha Noi. I still intended to deliver the portrait to your house the day I arrived, but in less than a week I lost myself in making new connections in the city. Intense memories of the front gradually faded away, and all the enthusiasm I had experienced out there waned. No, I don't blame the situation. I have to admit that, in this one instance, I alone was responsible. Soon receiving great praise from my most experienced colleagues for your portrait, I timidly avoided the mother who was living in the same city and anguishing over her son's reported death. Instead of seeing her, I packed the portrait for an exhibition overseas. On the pretext that I was short of time, I did not even think of paying your mother a visit!

There are times when people have no place to hide. So it was when I sat in the chair, my face turned upward, and recognized him beyond any doubt. I knew for sure that it was he. I only hoped that he would not remember me. But he surely did, for I have noticed, from looking at photos, that my face has not changed much in the past ten years. Worse, my face was only a few inches away from his. His eyes studied the face he held firmly in his hands. The skin on my face constricted sharply. I closed my eyes, then reopened them. Each time I opened them, I could not avoid looking at his. Oh my God, I must have sat on that barber's chair for half a century. What would he do?

You liar! Look! My mother wept herself blind. Now my portrait's appeared in art magazines all over the world and with your name honorably printed next to the words Portrait of a Liberation Soldier. *What celebrity!*

I am an artist, not a commercial portraitist. An artist's job is to serve many people, not a single individual. You're only an individual with your own individual troubles. You should understand that I had to put aside my promise so that I could serve the greater good. You must have seen that your portrait helped the whole world understand our war of resistance.

Ah-ha . . . Because of an artist's goal to serve the majority of people, you forgot me, deceived me? Get out of my sight! Clear out!

If only he had told me to hang about for a bit after the haircut, had questioned me about the promise I made eight years ago, then I would have never returned to the shop. But he acted as if he had never met me before. When I left, he was friendly and courteous; he politely said goodbye after collecting my money.

A month and a half passed, and I had not gotten another haircut. Often, I would ride my bicycle to the barbershop, but just as I approached, I would hastily speed up. I'd try to hide my face as I rushed by the shop, turning immediately onto another street for fear that his eyes might follow me. After this, I would head home, overwhelmed with disappointment. Other times, as I would draw near the shop, I would grow uncertain, hesitant. Then I would go to the refreshment stall in front of the hospital across the street. It was always crowded there. I would find a seat, order something, and watch the barbershop while sipping my drink. I always saw him there. His mother sometimes appeared, sometimes not.

Once, I didn't see him for two days. The shop was closed. On the third day, another woman was there, tidying up. I rushed in. The chair was gone, but the mirror and bottles remained. She asked me, "You come for a haircut, sir?"

"Yes, ma'am."

"My husband is moving to a new place on the other street. It's open tomorrow. Please come to our new shop."

His wife was about thirty years old; she had a gentle face. She talked to me while removing the picture.

"The portrait is nice, isn't it?" I said.

The woman blushed slightly, carefully rolling up the picture. After a moment, she said, "My husband said that the soldier in this picture was him when he was in Zone B, so he bought it and put it on the wall."

"That's what he told you?"

"Exactly."

"I was here a few days ago and saw an old woman . . ."

"It's my husband's mother. So you're a regular customer?"

"Yes . . . She went blind some time ago?"

"Yes, eight or nine years now."

"What was the reason?"

"She went blind on my husband's account. The day she learned that he was killed, she collapsed. He was her only child. She woke up at midnight and wandered about, crying inconsolably. She grieved over him so much."

"Do you know when that was?"

"In 1969."

"What month?"

"I don't remember exactly—around June, I think."

I had arrived in Ha Noi in March of that year. If I had kept my promise, she would not have gone blind. Moreover, I could have helped make her better. Was it I who had made her blind?

Many a time I walked into a very pleasant barbershop in my own neighborhood, one that I had often frequented; but after entering, I made one excuse after another to leave. Many a time I wanted to run away, but I always held back. I persuaded myself to accept the best solution: to not see the barber or his mother again. They had moved to another place. I had been recognized, and now was a good time to escape.

The hunter had turned on to another path, so why follow?

He didn't chase after me; it was my conscience that pursued me.

I was unable to flee . . . After years in the army he had resumed his old job, so he had to be in dire straits. I thought of collecting or borrowing a large sum of money equal to the income I had made from his portrait and then sending it to him. But no, that wouldn't work either. I could not allow myself to substitute money for repentance.

I rode out to his new place of business. His shop was near the intersection of an alley and a large road. Its location was a little better than the last, but it looked equally crude, except for the presence of a curtain. Once in a while, I would pass by and turn toward the curtain to listen for the sound of the clippers to catch a glimpse of the figure of the young man working behind it. Then I would push down hard on the pedal.

"The barber's moved out, hasn't he?" I feigned ignorance as I queried the tea-stall owner while sitting among the crowd of customers smoking and chatting.

"He has moved closer to the city center, a few blocks away. You must be a regular customer?"

"That's right."

"That barber is blessed to have such a helpful wife," one customer commented.

"Absolutely," the stall owner cut in. "When he was in the army, she took very good care of his mother when she was very ill. She cared for her as if she was a family member, although she was only a neighbor. When he returned, he appreciated her kindness and married her."

"God acts in strange and mysterious ways: he creates kindhearted people as well as treacherous villains."

My hair was now so long and bushy that my scalp itched unbearably. How did I become this crazy, torturing myself so? Why did I have to keep returning to that shop? That same morning I went back to the barbershop I had frequented for the past few years. The experience was a pleasant and relaxing one. The day was nice, not too sunny. The shop had a familiar feel; it was clean and smelled good. The barber commented that I must have been very busy, dropping in often but never having time to stay. The result was evident: my hair looked like a dense forest. He advised me not to work so much. I enjoyed chatting with him, as I normally do. I should say that he is the best barber in town. He works carefully, and he is one of my admirers. Acknowledging the privilege of serving a well-known painter, he worked carefully, weighing each movement of scissors and blade, and holding and touching my face and head the way he would a treasure.

And yet I didn't go back after that. The next time I needed a haircut, I decided to go to the other barbershop. I was determined to go in and not allow myself to run away any longer. I made up my mind to go there early one morning, when there would be only the two of us, so that he would have the opportunity to point at my face and say, "So you're the painter of that day? You made my mother weep until she was blind. OK, now sit down."

Through the curtain opening, I spotted the familiar objects: the chair, the clean white cloth draped over its back, the small table on which sat a bar of soap, the few bottles, the mirror above which was the portrait made eight years before. The barber was sitting with his back turned to me and one leg resting on the arm of the chair. He was eating sweet rice wrapped in a large, green leaf. His mother was there also, sitting on her heels and using a pestle to cram small bits of brick into cracks in the clay floor. The old woman looked up as she had the last time I was there, her face immobile and then turning bright.

"You come for a haircut, sir?"

"Yes, ma'am."

I felt the kind of excitement a soldier feels in the middle of an assault, when he has managed to cross the perimeter to break through the enemy's first line of defense. A few minutes before, I had ridden my bicycle near the shop and almost sped past, as I had done other times. *You come for a haircut, sir? Yes, ma'am.* Once again, if I had proved just a little more feeble in that micro-balance in my mind—if I had been just a little more cowardly, I would have answered "No, ma'am" instead of "Yes, ma'am," and then gotten on my bicycle and rushed away, as I had done before.

Hearing what his mother said, the barber turned around and saw me. I could see in his eyes—eyes that still appeared young—a look that was at first questioning, then surprised, and then serious. In the blink of an eye, the reactions passed across his face. In a second, he regained his modest, warm demeanor—the appearance of an honest and devoted barber.

The skin of my face seemed to tighten as I braced myself.

"Will you sit down please?"

I tried to control myself so as not to tremble, but I sat down in the chair as if it were wired for a police interrogation.

"Do you want it cut in the same way?"

"Yes."

His hand pushed my neck down, and I could see his old army pants and rubber sandals. His mother was still sitting by the chair, striking the pestle on pieces of broken brick. Some strokes hit their target, others missed.

Locks of hair fell down from my head. I had the impression that I was undergoing a neurological operation without anesthesia.

Holding a shiny razor in his hand, the barber then tilted my face upward. I glanced and noticed that it was sharp, and yet he sharpened it further on a piece of leather. I was waiting impatiently. I moved my neck slightly, and it felt as if it had been bolted to the back of the chair. In the mirror in front of me was my real face, free of its daily mask.

The barber spoke. "Every day you tell your friends a good joke: that the creator made each species with a different kind of dough. The work having been done, the creator gathered all the scraps and made you out of them. Right?"

"Maybe that's right, and in me there exist both the good and bad, the noble and wicked, angels and devils."

"Now tell me what you think of the law of justice in your own life: do you get what you give?"

"I admit that I've brought your mother great sorrow. I've deceived you. I've profited with both money and fame from your agony. Now you could punish me. I'll accept your judgment."

"Never. If I had punished you, if I had practiced that law of yours, I would have thrown you down the brook amid the cat's ear stones when I turned back that day eight years ago."

"So you'll treat me the same way you did last time?"

"Definitely."

"You won't criticize or accuse me?"

"No, don't worry. I've always considered you a talented artist who has much to contribute to society."

"When did you recognize me? When I first came to your barbershop?"

"I've seen you often on the street. Once I saw you sketching the old town; another time I went to your exhibition. And another time I went with some friends who worked in the TV station to film your studio and apartment. You couldn't recognize me then."

"Now tell me something. Advise me what to do."

"No."

"Should I just slink away?"

"No. You can come back. I'll give you the best care—you know it."

Yes, that's right. If the barber had lost his temper and chased me out of his shop on my first or second visit or on any of the subsequent ones, I would not have had enough time to examine my own face closely. For over half a year now, I have poured all my efforts and thoughts into this painting. During that time, I have tried to hint at the old incident a few times, but the barber always behaves as if he had never met me before. Back home as a barber, or in wartime as a soldier, he leads a quiet life, letting people judge their deeds by themselves. His advice is, "Everybody, please suspend your busy, hustling lifestyle for a minute and think about yourselves."

Now that my latest work is completed, I must come face-to-face with myself and write these words down as a commentary on a piece of art that depicts a very large human face. As if emanating from thousands of candles, beams of light fall on the dense growth of hair that covers one-half of the head like a dark and mysterious forest. At first glimpse, the other half looks very much like a human brain: the skin is peeled back from the head and the flesh exposed, as if left open in an operation. The lower part of the face seems hidden beneath a mask: the chin, jaws, and corners of the lips are concealed under lather. The mouth is not clearly visible except as a fuzzy, dark spot floating on a sea of white foam. Standing out sharply against that face are the eyes: wide open, restless, worried, stern . . . focused deep on the inner self.

Translation by Nguyen Thi Kieu Thu and Kevin Bowen

145. COCHINCHINE — Cholon – Pagode nouvelle

FRANK GERKE

Our Hands Shall Embrace:
A Eulogy for Trinh Cong Son

Woods and mountains reach out their hands
To reunite with the faraway sea.
We form a large circle
To reunite with the woods and mountains.
In this endless country
My brothers and sisters meet again,
In happiness like a sandstorm
Swirling round and round in this infinity.
And our hands shall embrace Viet Nam.
        "Noi vong tay lon" (Let's form a big circle)

He sang these words live at noon on 30 April 1975 at a Saigon radio station just when the Northern liberation army marched into town. And he meant what he said. Not only in this song, but also in many others, he expressed his great hope for peace and love—a hope he saw related to the liberation of Saigon. He felt sure that, after this moment, there would be a new Viet Nam—a Viet Nam without death, hate, murder, suffering, and expulsion. The "he" I refer to is Trinh Cong Son, the singer, poet of love and peace, and conscience of Viet Nam.

Like no one else, Trinh Cong Son portrayed the horrible face of the war and sang about it to decadent Saigon society. In doing this, he became the most famous singer-songwriter of Viet Nam. He was persecuted by the old Saigon regime like nobody else, but for him, the horror of the war did not exist on one side of the line alone. He showed that its horrible and brutal face existed on the other side as well. The new leaders in Ha Noi disliked his songs, perhaps because he did not sing about the heroic battles for the liberation of the Vietnamese people; Son did not deny this fact. In the opinion of the new government, he did not fit in ideologically, and so, shortly after his April 1975 appearance on the radio, he was forced to do self-criticism on the same station. Afterwards, the government condemned him to four years of reeducation camp.

Trinh Cong Son was born on 28 February 1939 in Lac Giao (now called Buon Ma Thuot), Dac Lac Province, in the Central Highlands, and died at the age of sixty-two on 1 April 2001 in Cho Ray Hospital, Ho Chi Minh City, after a long battle with diabetes. Though born in Dac Lac Province, Son had his family home in Hue. After graduation from Rousseau High School, he studied pedagogy in Quy Nhon and earned his first living as a teacher in the Central Highlands. He had loved music from early child-hood, but it was not until he lived in the seclusion of the highlands that he wrote his first compositions. In the beginning, he never thought of becoming a professional musician. He once said, "I did not start composing music in order to do it as a profession. I remember that I wrote my first songs because of feelings deep inside myself. That was around 1956 or 1957—a time of confusing dreams and useless, silly fantasies. It was the time of youth—a youth fresh and green like the fruits at the beginning of the season. I really loved music very much, but never intended to become a musician."

In 1958, Son wrote "Uot mi" (Moist eyelashes), a slow, sad ballad that became his first success. It was published by An Phu Publishing House in Saigon in 1959. At his residence in Saigon, Son once told me that he had been paid two thousand Indochinese *piaster*s for that song. Fifteen hun-dred *piaster*s he gave to his family, and five hundred he kept to go out dancing. In those times, one needed only about fifty *piaster*s to take a girl out for dinner and dancing. His next big success came in 1959 with "Thuong mot nguoi" (To love somebody).

In the years that followed, Trinh Cong Son appeared on stage frequently and his music became especially successful with the younger generation. In 1962 he went to Da Lat, where he met a female singer named Mai, who went under the stage name Khanh Ly. In her voice, Son found something extra-ordinary: something completely different from anything he had heard before. "I had a very exceptional feeling. When I heard her singing and saw how she moved on stage, I knew that this was the singer best suited for my music."

He persuaded Khanh Ly to go back with him to Saigon. Together, both became famous. But then the war broke out. Son went to the front and was deeply shocked by what he saw: cruelty, hatred, and suffering. Soon after-wards, he began to write his antiwar songs: "Noi vong tay lon" (Let's form a big circle), "Gia tai cua me" (Family treasure of the mother), "Cho mot nguoi nam xuong" (To someone killed in action). These and many more spoke to a whole generation faced with the horror of war. Abroad, Son became well known as the Bob Dylan of Viet Nam. In April 1975, the war ended with the fall of Saigon and the liberation of South Viet Nam. Panic-stricken, many people left the country—among them Khanh Ly, other famous artists, and Son's family. But Trinh Cong Son stayed. Much later he would say, "You cannot replant a Vietnamese tree somewhere else; it will die. I stayed because I wanted to take responsibility for my people."

In the 1980s, after Son's music had been banned for almost a decade by the government of the reunited Viet Nam, the authorities permitted him to participate again in the cultural life of the country. With the exception of the greater part of his antiwar songs—beloved by many—his songs could be played. He enjoyed great success, perhaps even greater than before, and started writing new songs, most of them philosophical. As the essayist Hoang Phu Ngoc Tuong observed in 1998, Son "used his soul to live together with the people again." In "Mot coi di ve" (Everlasting return home), Son wrote:

> A loving ghost suddenly called
> And once again I see that inside myself
> The human shadow has appeared

In Son's songs, joy and sorrow always coexist, as well as rain and sunshine, sun and moon, day and night. These images alternate with each other endlessly. Songs like "Toi oi, dung tuyet vong" (Don't despair, my soul), "Chiec la thu phai" (A fading autumn leaf), "Bong khong la bong" (The bong-fish is not a fish), and "Trong noi dau tinh co" (Suddenly hurt) are so well known that one can hear them almost everywhere. Son's "Song ve dau" (Where are the waves going?) became a number-one hit in 1999. A CD release of this song in 2000 received the prize for best CD of the year. Also that year, Son and saxophonist Tran Manh Tuan appeared on stage before a cheering crowd and sang the last song he ever wrote: "Tien thoai luong nan" (Going onward or backward—both impossible). He sang as if to announce his own approaching death.

In the last years of his life, Son did not write many songs, but he composed music on a regular basis. He liked to perform on many occasions, and he went on tour to France, Canada, Singapore, and Japan, where he had been awarded gold records as early as 1972. In the 1990s, his works came to be regarded as timeless: he reached all generations, from people who listened to him in his early days to the current generation.

Son is widely respected as the father of modern Vietnamese song. However, his compositions are not only songs; they are also regarded as poems by the nation's literary experts and critics, as they were by Son himself. In all, he composed about seven hundred songs, among them many that were hits in other countries as well.

His untimely "painful and heartless death"—a phrase from "Nguoi con gai Viet Nam da vang" (The Vietnamese girl with the yellow skin)—created a great shock wave among those who knew and loved him, either through his music or as a friend. In his song "Tinh ca cua nguoi mat tri" (Love song of a girl who lost her mind), he offered a different explanation of how death comes: "Death appears unexpectedly / one is lying down and it is as if in a dream."

Son wrote and sang a lot about death. And in these songs, he presented a view of life based, on one hand, on Buddhism and, on the other hand, on his existentialist philosophy:

> Once I was lying down and had a dream
> And in my dream I saw myself dying,
> And even though I shed one small tear,
> I was not especially sad about it.
>
> "Ben doi hiu quanh" (A quiet life)

> How many years a human life lasts,
> One afternoon we suddenly realize our hair is white as lime,
> Withered leaves falling down,
> And even if we're given one hundred years,
> One day we still must die.
>
> "Cat bui" (Dust)

Unfortunately, Trinh Cong Son did not live to a hundred, although he very much would have wanted to. He loved this life and enjoyed it to the fullest. In "Toi oi, dung tuyet vong" (Don't despair, my soul), he sang, "Who am I, still crying now and then? / Who am I, still firmly rooted in this world? / Who am I, who am I, loving this life so much?" In "Moi ngay toi chon mot niem vui" (Each day I choose something to enjoy), he said explicitly, "I love this life with all of my heart."

In his antiwar songs, he sang not only about death, but also about life. In "Gia tai cua me" (Family treasure of the mother), he noted with irony that "A thousand years enslaved by the Chinese, / a hundred years oppressed by the Westerners, / the family property the mother leaves to her children is the sad country Viet Nam." In "Cho mot nguoi nam xuong" (To someone killed in action), he described the suffering of a girl whose lover, a pilot, was shot down; and in "Tinh ca cua nguoi mat tri," he told of the despair of a girl who lost her boyfriends, one after the other, on the cruel battlefields of the Central Highlands jungles:

> I had a lover who fell in the battle of Pleime
> I had a lover who died in war zone D
> He fell in the battle of Dong Xoai
> People die in Ha Noi,
> Die oh so suddenly all along the border.

Son's antiwar songs describe the pure facts of war; they are never ideological. He never engaged in politics because that was simply not his objective in life. But he dared to speak up and tell people about the negative and harmful consequences of human behavior. Without pointing the finger directly at any individual, he accused all those who called themselves leaders—all those who, through misguided convictions and blind ideology, tried to impose their beliefs on others. Such convictions misled hundreds of thousands and caused the deaths of millions.

Some of Son's songs ask his people to resist; for example, "Hay song dum toi" (Live together with me) or "Noi vong tay lon." But in these songs, there are no real politics. Many people thought the latter song was a summons to resist the ambitions of the West in Viet Nam, but that was never Son's intention. He wanted the Vietnamese to become brothers and sisters, to reconcile in order to build a new, peaceful Viet Nam. If this is taken into consideration, the line "From north to south, let's all join hands" cannot be understood as a request for the North to conquer the South. However, in the 1960s and 1970s, "Noi vong tay lon" became the battle hymn of the student movement protesting war, aggression, and oppression from outside South Viet Nam. Today it is the official hymn of the Students' Association.

In Viet Nam as well as other places, Son was known and loved for his open-mindedness and honesty as well as his great music. He could never bring himself to utter bad words or to shout. It was true when he sang this line from "Van nho cuoc doi" (I still remember life): "One day I suddenly realized that I love all people." In his 2 April obituary, his friend, the author Nguyen Quang Sang, noted: "Even about a friend who, for whatever reason, had turned his back upon him, he could sing sincerely, with a heart filled with tremendous love." Son could never be angry with anybody. And when he thought that it wasn't worth talking about a thing anymore, he would say, *"Thoi ke"* (Enough of that).

His funeral was attended by tens of thousands, and hundreds of thousands gathered along the road running from his house in Saigon to his last resting place: the Go Dua cemetery, in the Quag Binh Pagoda, twenty kilometers outside of the city. For three days, his casket was placed on a bier, and countless mourners paid him their last respects. Despite the tense relationship that had existed between him and the political leaders of the country, many well-known politicians paid their condolences to his family. Among them were the family of former premier Vo Van Kiet and representatives of the People's Committee of Ho Chi Minh City. Other mourners included two beggars on crutches and ten young Buddhist monks, who sang one of his songs at his grave. When tens of thousands spontaneously started singing "Cat bui," "Cho mot nguoi nam xuong," "Mot coi di ve," and "Noi vong tay lon" to the playing of the country's top saxophonist, Tran Manh Tuan, it was clear that the whole nation was saying good-bye to a hero.

Trinh Cong Son once said of himself, "I am only a simple street singer, leading a vagabond life and moving around the country in order to express our dreams of this illusory life."

Son, we miss you so much. We love you as the friend and artist you were, and we promise to hold you in honor forever!

Editor's note: The following songs by Trinh Cong Son were translated by Nguyen Qui Duc.

YOU WALK IN THE AFTERNOON

You cross the bridge
A wind follows
Blowing the white mourning cloth
In the framed afternoon.

You cross the bridge
Leaves rustle
Above the deep river
Carrying a wounded soul.

You cross the bridge
Carrying the afternoon on shoulders
Holding sadness between lips
The heart is tired
Someone has lain down
Someone remains.

You cross the bridge
Your soul in the clouds
You walk in the afternoon
A life of mourning
Longing alone for one.

You cross the bridge
The gunshot echoing still
The village seems rather sad.

You cross the bridge
A soft wind
Blows your heart
Away into the distance.

UNKNOWN ORIGINS

You pass by on a boat
Catching the moon asleep
The river is an inn
And the moon's a traveler
You pass by on a boat
Catching the moon still young

The river does not know
One day the moon will age.

You pass by on a boat
The moon is old now
The moon is forever in debt
But the river has forgotten
You pass by on a boat
Listening to the river telling its tale
Moon, you're very bad
If you go, come back soon
Come back soon if you go.

You pass by on a boat
Joyful as if in a festival
I shall be the waiting inn
For you to drop by in boredom
You pass by this place
Why so hurried?
I shall be a pebble
Rolling after your footsteps.

I'm at play in life
Not knowing my roots
The tree's shadow shortens at noon
I shrink into darkness
I'm at play in life
Not knowing my roots
I shrink myself
And turn into raindrops
Disappearing in the sky.

SINGING OVER THE BODIES

Going up to the high hills in the afternoon
Singing over the dead bodies
I have seen, I have seen on the road
People carrying each other in escape.
Going up to the high hills in the afternoon
Singing over the dead bodies
I have seen, I have seen by the courtyard
A mother holding the body of her child.

Mother claps her hands cheering her child's body
Mother claps her hands rejoicing peace

Someone claps his hands to add to the beat
Another claps his hands
Keeping rhythm for the sufferings.

Passing by Bai Dau in the afternoon
Singing over the dead bodies
I have seen, I have seen on the road
An old father holding his child's cold body.
Passing by Bai Dau in the afternoon
Singing over the dead bodies
I have seen, I have seen the graves
Holding my brothers' bodies

Mother claps her hands cheering war
Sister claps her hands rejoicing peace
Someone claps his hands to add to vengeance
Another claps his hands
Turning away from repentance.

SONG FOR THE BODIES

A body floats on the river,
Drying on the fields,
Lying on the city's roofs,
On the winding streets.
A lonely body lies,
Under the eave of the temple,
In the city's church,
On the deserted porch.
Spring, these bodies will give scent to the fields.
Viet Nam, these bodies will give life to tomorrow's soil.
Even if the roads ahead are full of drudgery,
There will be these bodies around here.
Bodies lying around here in the cold rain,
Next to the old and frail bodies,
There are those still innocent.
Which of these is my little one,
In these graves,
In the burning spots,
By the beds of corn and potato?
Bodies lie next to each other,
Hanging from bridges,
In a corner of a ruined house,
Down the deep trenches.

Bodies now are only dried bones
Behind the empty alleys,
On the uneven paths uphill.
Tomorrow these bodies will feed growing trees,
All over these fields.
Tomorrow,
The bodies will sing as clumps of fresh hay,
To new rice fields,
People will go out,
Building their future with full hands.

FROM AGES AGO

I can still spot you
In a crowd of strangers
Because you carry in your eyes
Your eternal love for life.

I can still spot you
In a crowd of strangers
Because in those eyes
Rest the nation and friends.

You've appeared in our nation
Carrying the years of long ago
In your body,
So I can still spot you
In a crowd of strangers;
You are like the white bird
Stepping out from the bronze drum.

I can still spot you
In a crowd of strangers
Because you are like flowers and leaves
In tender nature.

from *Foreeel*

Editor's Note

Since the late 1970s, writers in Hawai'i have experimented with ways to create literature using the local Creole English known as Pidgin. This oral language developed in the early twentieth century among laborers who had immigrated to the islands to work on the sugar plantations. Speaking Chinese, Japanese, and Portuguese, among other languages, these workers created a *lingua franca*—rich with their various vocabularies, syntaxes, and speech rhythms—which is still used throughout the islands.

One of the challenges Hawai'i's Pidgin authors face is the difficulty of putting into writing this fundamentally oral language—where meaning is conveyed experientially, by nuances of pitch and rhythm, by tone and gesture, or by an eyebrow's inflection.

Bradajo (also known as Jozuf Hadley) has been at the forefront of Pidgin poetry since his first book/record, *Chalookyu eensai,* was released in 1972. His approach to affixing language to the page remains unique among Pidgin authors. He sidesteps rules of orthography, syntax, and punctuation. Instead, his robust, good-humored calligraphic renderings of sounds ripple across the white field, recreating the play and surprise of speech.

Readers may listen to Bradajo reciting the following poems by visiting the *Mānoa* web page at www.hawaii.edu/mjournal/text/vietnam02.html.

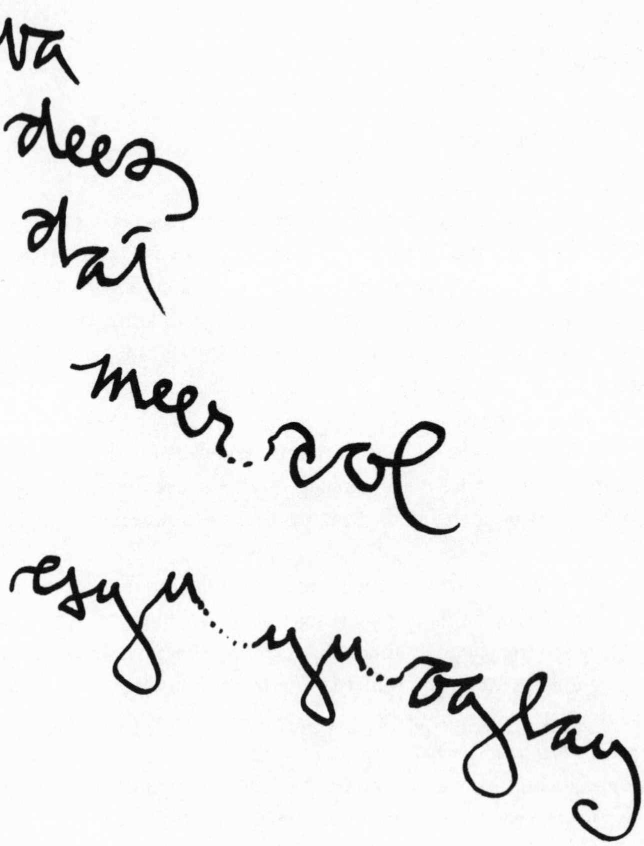

oss...hed...ax
da...sac...ken
kwas...chen
bicos

oss...hed...fogel
da...frrs...kwas...chen
eef...oss...remamba
da...frrs...kwas...chen

oss...nonee
ax...kwas...chen

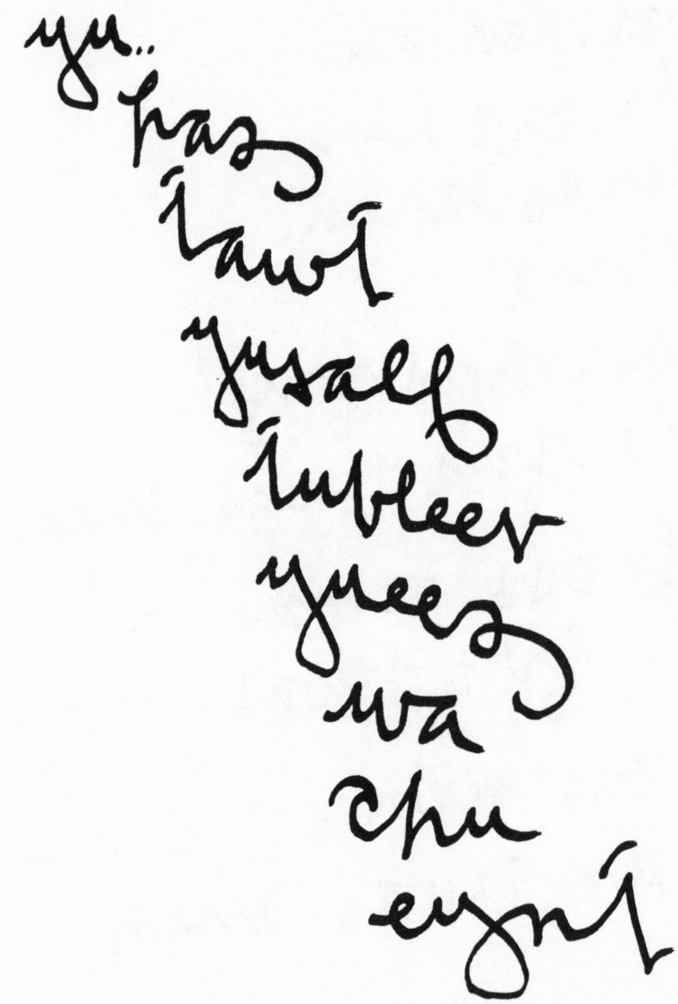

bicos
yu...eint
no...no
yu...eint
huyu
teenkuyu

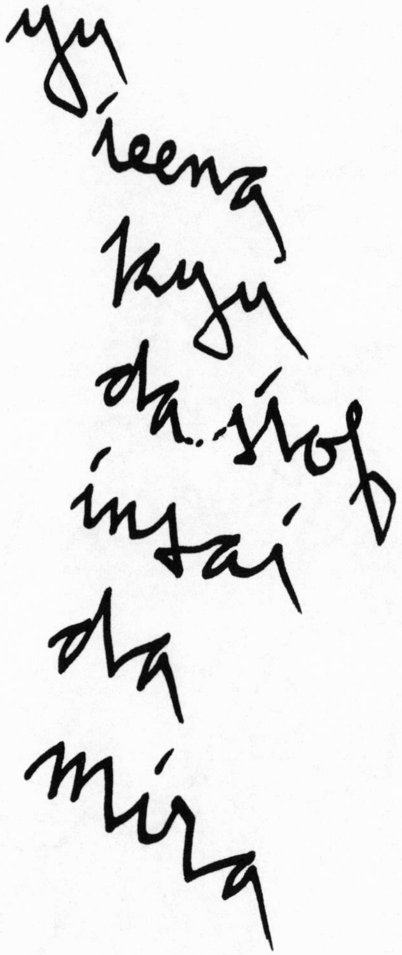
yu
da
insai
da
mira

we
ees
awl
holimen
hu..wen
fogel
aua
holiness

Selling Out at the Top of the World _____

for John

Nobody spoke in the Arctic cold those mornings we rode
over wrecked lunar fields following tracks to the dynamite shed.
        Not the drillers from Oklahoma in ski masks
and insulated coveralls, not the Eskimos from Barrow,
some wearing only down vests and flannel; not even us,
        the survey helpers, tears and snot
                from the freezing wind lacing our faces in ice.

We'd screw the cans of explosive together, load the steel chain
and transit and start driving north to the line,
        where leads of dark sea water
flexed through the ice like a wound that refused to heal.
Scrabbling across sloped pressure ridges and planting
        wire flags in the crust,
we knew our charts would be sold to Nixon's cohorts,
Exxon and Richfield, that the Revolution had come north
        to freeze and die under the waters of Prudhoe Bay.

                Scattered across the north slope
of the Brooks Range, countless gypsy seismograph crews
        scratched and gouged in twilit shadows,
prospecting the ocean floor. The ice where we lived grew
six feet thick over the Beaufort Sea, and we clustered like flies
        at the top of the world, watching the sun
creep like a slow fuse partway around the horizon, soft light shining
back from the surface, hanging the air with ghosts—
        mountains upside down
at our feet, white buildings hovering half out of the sea,
and the moon on its back, refusing to set
                over the ragged plains.

If our hearts had been pure we'd have grieved
                for ourselves or found other wages farther south.
Instead we surrendered to spasms of laughter in the anesthetic cold,
                making up names for the Texas bosses—
Black Jack, Sidewinder, Big Tomato—planning the movie
we'd someday write, a *noir*-Western starring Richard Widmark's
                pale narrow eyes and rictus grin.

Wyatt Earp and Jim Bowie had nothing down on our Okie drillers,
who'd flown here from the Middle East with stories
                we listened to evenings,
of jewelled Arabian sunsets
or the withering sandstorms of Egypt, where Moslem laborers
        were called back to work as they knelt
in their daily prayers,
                        by numbers they wore on their backs.

Here we only stopped work to wolf candy bars
            or piss in the frozen tracks of the boom truck.
Nobody wanted to say much about home, though one spoke
of the Sacramento delta where he'd worked as a brakeman
            for Southern Pacific, gone to high school
with the Mitchell brothers before they became pornography kings.
Some were here to escape other lives, ex-wives and children,
            jail time down south,
many just back from Viet Nam. Who knew if they'd watched the live
demonstrations where people like us dodged tear gas, the walls
            of our communal houses on fire
with Che Guevara's austere face or the black thunderbird of
    Cesar Chavez?
            Here the Indians never looked
straight at anyone, and the stiff wings of winter closed
down on us all, as though we'd been born without histories
            to this godless landscape of ice and bent light.

When we got loose in town we paid whores from LA a hundred extra
to dine with us in the Gold Rush Room of the Anchorage Westin Hotel.
I fell quickly in love with mine, her black nails sparkling
      like onyx rain
as she turned her wrist to look at her watch.
They harvested our amnesiac wages the way pipeliners
      empty an oil field.
None could wait to sell out for a fortune, be rid of the sixties'
experiments—ecology, brotherhood, socialism—except maybe
      the cook from Baton Rouge,
who'd lost fifteen grand playing dice at the Embers
and wanted us to help get it back.

      Not much would ever be given back
to the wilderness beginning to crack and thaw over the bright seams
of moonlight near the drilling rigs on the sea. Not the underground
      swamp gas rising through cleavages
forced apart by the drills, not the patches of tundra scarred
by surveyors trying to leave tracks in the storm,
      not even the ridges of this winter's ice,
          glowing like quartz in the tractor lamps.

When we returned, camp was moving again, exhaust fumes
hanging the air like a shroud, two D-8 Cats towing trailers on sleds
      over ashen terrain toward Canada.
We watched from above in the company chopper, hovering over
the dim caravan, eating chocolate and taking swigs of scotch,
      the smell of death frozen into the night,
fuel oil, diesel smoke, leaf mold predating the kingdom
of Solomon, the collapsed insides of the dinosaur,
      the decomposed skull of the mastodon
turning the cold steel rotors of time
          under the blind April stars.

VIET THANH NGUYEN

Better Homes and Gardens

The boy decided he was in a time warp. No computers, no AC, no FM radio, no security cameras. High tech for the motel was the neon sign outside blinking VACANCY, and the last guest had signed the motel clerk's ledger two weeks ago.

The clerk's name was Ramirez, and the boy could swear he saw a fine blanket of cobwebs tying him to his chair. As Ramirez copied the information from the boy's driver's license into his ledger, he made no secret of the fact that he found the boy and the girl interesting.

Avoiding the clerk's glances, the boy studied the walls of the office, which looked like they had been painted with a toothbrush. The most remarkable thing about the walls were the black-and-white pictures hanging on them. Even though he was squinting, the boy couldn't make out the details of the pictures.

"What are those of? The moon?"

"Looks like it, don't it?" Ramirez smiled eagerly. "That's my hobby. I like finding places that look like they don't belong here. On Earth, I mean. That's a dry lake bed; those are sand dunes; that's a piece of petrified wood, up close."

"Oh."

"Yeah, I'm a photographer." From under the counter, the clerk pulled out a battle-scarred 35 mm Leica. "My next series is people. The people who pass through this motel."

"That can't be a lot of people." The girl was leaning against the counter next to the boy, hiding behind her sunglasses. With her eyes hidden, the girl was not just pretty but beautiful, in an affordable way.

"But that's what makes it interesting." Ramirez pounded on the counter with his fist. "Who the hell stops here? That's what I want to know."

"Makes two of us." The girl wandered to the window, her jackboots clicking on the tile floor. The sun was setting. Sunset, the boy thought, must be nature's way of having mercy on the landscape. It was an ashen, exhausted place, useful only for testing nuclear bombs and burying murder victims.

"A lot of them look like they don't belong nowhere." Ramirez's voice

171

trailed off. He and the boy contemplated each other in silence, and the boy wondered how he would look mounted on the clerk's wall. It might be fun to be the first person in the photographer's series. Fun but not smart.

"Maybe another time." The boy picked up the room key.

Ramirez flashed his eager smile again. "I'm still here if you change your mind," he called out as they left, but the only answer to his invitation was the tiny bell that rung at the pair's exit.

Their room, the boy decided, was strictly Third World. Rag-thin towels, originally white but now the shade of a light suntan. Styrofoam cups but no coffee maker and no tea, just fresh tap water. A thirteen-inch television, color but no cable. The wire antenna picked up static and news anchors who looked like beet farmers. A comforter of vertigo-inducing plaid invited guests to pass out on the double-sized bed.

"He's creepy." Lighting a cigarette, the girl flopped on the bed, not bothering to pull down her leather skirt when it hiked up her thighs. "When's Number One supposed to get here? I'm bored stupid already."

"He's probably lost." The boy sat down on the bed next to her and put his hand on her warm thigh. They had known each other for exactly two days and two hours since he had picked her up in Seattle as part of his cargo, due for delivery to Los Angeles. In his world and hers, two days was a very long time, and neither gave very much thought to what happened next. The girl had a reputation among the johns for being something special, and he found out why. She was like an alien in a science-fiction movie pumping him for blood, and after a while he thought his head would explode. He saw a dim reflection of himself in the sunglasses she kept on, and he liked what he saw: a body as thin and taut as a razor-scarred leather strop.

When they were done having sex, they lay next to each other, naked and quiet. The fantasy crept back into his mind and he tried to brush it away, but there it was: the two of them drinking almond hazelnut coffee from cups made of blue enameled china and laughing over something while sitting in a breakfast nook lined in maple wood and illuminated with clean and precious sunlight pouring in through French windows. He had cribbed the details from an advertisement in *Better Homes and Gardens* for instant coffee. While his friends flipped through *Lowrider* and *Soldier of Fortune* in the magazine aisle of Borders, he hid the *Better Homes and Gardens* behind the pages of a *Playboy* and wondered what a freshly brewed cup of Yuban smelled like in the morning.

"Got a smoke?" When he handed her a cigarette, she shook her head and took off her sunglasses. "The other kind."

While she lit the joint, he saw that she looked somewhat out of focus, the way most pretty girls did when their makeup was smudged after having sex or crying. She returned his gaze with the kind of scrutiny people save for a hundred-dollar bill.

"So what do those stand for?" She pointed at the five blue Ts tattooed in a vertical line on his right bicep.

"*Tinh, Tien, Tu, Toi, Thu.*" Flexing the bicep, he pointed at each T as he gave its meaning. "Love, money, prison, guilt, revenge."

"A whole life story." She took a drag. "What about those?" There were five black scars on his left forearm, arranged like the five dots on a gambling die.

"Cigarette burns. One for every man I killed."

She laughed. "That's a good joke." When she saw him scowl, she stopped laughing. "You're tough, aren't you?"

"What do you think?" He slipped out of bed and went to the bathroom.

"I think luck is tough," she replied. "You, I don't know."

"No, you don't know."

In reality there was only one man, and that was an accident. The boy's gun was a snake in a cage, twisting about and snapping its neck every which way, and he shot the wrong one, leaving him bleeding and screaming under a pool table. It was luck he even hit the man he did, but he couldn't admit that; he had to say the poor bastard got in his way. While he urinated, he practiced his scowl in the mirror. Psychological warfare, Number One called it. You can't kill a man unless your looks can kill. The boy always tried to pay attention to the lessons that Number One taught, because he liked to please Number One and he knew what might happen if Number One got mad.

When he came out of the bathroom, he saw that the girl was dressed and, high as she was, reapplying her makeup with quick, efficient strokes. He paused to admire her work before pulling his clothes on and tucking his gun in the back of his pants.

"Thirsty?"

"Like a desert." She turned the compact so she could see him in the mirror. "Be a sweetie."

His sense of paranoia compelled him to check on the Nova. He had picked up the car for a thousand dollars in cash. With fifty thousand tabs of Dutch-imported Ecstasy hidden in it, the Nova was now worth a million on the street. Its doors were locked and its windows rolled up, and he gave the Nova, which he had nicknamed the Love Bug, an affectionate pat.

He walked past the eleven other rooms, all vacant, before he reached the clerk's office at the other end of the motel. Outside the office was a vending machine, which he slipped a dollar into and then punched for water. When nothing happened, he punched the button again.

Ramirez poked his head out the door when he heard the boy kicking the machine.

"That won't do no good."

"It took my money."

"I got a form you can fill out. You'll get your money in a few weeks."

"Forget it." The boy felt his empty pockets. "Can I bum a cigarette?"

"Sure." Ramirez grinned and beckoned him in. "I got some bad scotch, too."

They sat down on the couch behind the counter. Ramirez sniffed the air in the boy's direction before pulling out a bottle of scotch from under the counter. The boy ignored the hint and the empty bottle of scotch that Ramirez had apparently already drunk. He smoked one of the clerk's cigarettes and looked around the office, focusing on one of the pictures he hadn't noticed before.

"I know that one," he said. "The pyramids."

"Amazing, huh?"

"Yeah, but everybody knows the pyramids are on this planet."

"Sure they're on this planet." Ramirez staggered up from the sofa with the bottle of scotch in one hand and a glass in the other. He hesitated for a second and then put the glass down. "But who put them here?"

"The Egyptians."

"Some people say aliens." Ramirez stumbled over to the picture and tapped on it with a hardened finger. "That's how we came here, supposedly. Aliens landed and built the pyramids. Left us behind, too."

"You believe that?"

"I believe we can believe anything." Ramirez leaned against the wall and drank straight from the bottle. "Like my ancestors. The Indians. The idiots thought the Spanish were gods when they washed up here. We coulda killed them on the beach."

"Coulda, shoulda."

"Not gods." Ramirez took another drink and slid snail-like down the wall. "Just bastards with guns."

The boy took his time finishing his drink. Ramirez started to snore so loudly that his teeth clattered in his head. Grimacing, the boy rose, patted him on the shoulder, and left.

Once he was outside the office, his cell phone rang. The ringer was set to Beethoven's Fifth Symphony because the boy liked the opening notes: the hand of God knocking on a door.

"Yeah."

"Stockyards." Number One sounded annoyed. "Cows far as I can see."

"You're close. Follow the smell."

The girl was still in bed, watching a fuzzy version of *Planet of the Apes*. His car keys were clipped to a Swiss army knife, and he could feel their weight in his pocket. He tossed them onto the nightstand and thought about the astronauts in the movie being orphans, just like the girl and he were. The girl had said her mother was a Saigon bar girl, her father a ROK who had gone back to South Korea when his tour of duty was done. The bitch, as she described her mother, married a GI and dumped her on a doorstep in Wichita, Kansas, six months after their arrival in the States.

"Sorry, lady. No agua at this hotel."

"Great. Looks like a desert, feels like a desert." The girl got up and went to the bathroom tap for water. "Why does he want to meet us out here, for God's sake?"

"I don't know. He doesn't tell me everything."

"You just follow orders." She stood in the doorway of the bathroom, sipping from a Styrofoam cup. "Is he an egomaniac, with a name like that?"

"He's got a thing for *Star Trek*."

"Excuse me?"

"You know, Mr. Spock—he's Number One on the ship."

"I get the picture. He's a freak."

"He's not a freak. He's just got imagination."

"Trust me, he's a freak." The girl crumpled the cup and rolled it into a ball. "I've heard about some of the things you guys do to people."

"Us guys?"

"What, you're not involved in all this?"

Of course he was involved. Not with Number One's whorehouses—not yet—but in the home invasions, he was Number One's point man. Home invasions were their bread-and-butter, better than an ATM when they needed money quick. The fact that home invasions required beating old people, tying down little girls, and putting guns to the heads of hysterical mothers did not bother him, for as far as he was concerned, they deserved it all. What they didn't deserve were their money and their love when he had neither, but he didn't say this to the girl, pausing instead for a moment to swallow the rage that was backing up in his throat so thick that he wanted to hawk it up and spit it on someone. When he had choked the rage down, he mumbled, "We all gotta do what we gotta do."

"You don't want to do anything else?" She sat down on the bed.

"Like what?"

At first he thought she lowered her head and hid her face out of disgust over his lack of imagination, but then she started to shake, just a little at first and then faster and harder. She was beginning to cry, and he knew he was supposed to say and do something, but he was paralyzed by the fact that everything he could think of seemed as prepackaged as a Big Mac.

When he did sit down next to her, she folded under his arm neatly and easily, which surprised him. He had never held a girl this way, and it was unexplored territory. It wasn't so much what she might do that worried him but what he might do.

"It's OK." He winced as he said it, but she didn't see him.

"No, it's not. I don't want to go with him."

"He takes good care of his girls."

"I'm tired of someone taking care of me."

"That doesn't make sense." He paused. "I'd like someone to take care of me." Once spoken, the words sounded awful and artificial to him, like muzak or the Lawrence Welk polka he had once seen on television in another motel room. The words were true, nonetheless, and while he wondered what strange, dark garden in his soul they were coming from, she didn't seem to notice that what he said was bizarre in any way.

"You've got too little and I've got too much." She took his hand, and in her mouth the words sounded right. "Together we'd have just enough."

The plan she proposed was simple. Number One was coming with two bodyguards to take her and the Ecstasy. The boy would stand outside the motel and greet them when they arrived, waving them into a spot next to the clerk's pickup. After they got out of the car, facing him, she would come from behind the pickup with the boy's gun and start firing, taking out two before the third got his gun. This one the boy could tackle from behind.

It could work. That was his first thought, and it sent a deep thrill of excitement through him, a feeling as vivid and dangerous as what he imagined he would feel if he saw his parents again—dangerous because the excitement was a drill digging into his guts and he was scared of what might come out. Yes, the concept of the plan was clear and appealing to him, and her hand, which was now squeezing his thigh, reminded him of rewards beyond drugs and money. But the plan was theoretical and Number One was real.

"What about Ramirez?"

"I guess he has to go, too." The girl frowned in concentration. "No one's going to miss him for a while."

She stood up and paced the length of the bed, back and forth. The sight of her flawless thighs, windowed between the miniskirt and the jackboots, mesmerized him. He wanted to slide his hand between those thighs again, where her blood flowed hot and close to the surface.

"We've got to get the Mexican first." She stopped in front of him, decisive. "Otherwise he'll call for help."

He shifted on the bed and felt the hard edge of the gun against his back.

"Number One's almost here."

"I can't do it without you." Throwing herself on the bed, she almost landed on his lap. He felt a teardrop on his hand. "And if I can't do it, I'm going back to that life. This life."

He thought about all the places she had been and told him about. Arlington, Philadelphia, Minneapolis, Houston, Dallas, Chicago, New York, Honolulu, Seattle. Next stop, until a few hours ago, Los Angeles. A few months in each place, never staying long enough to wear out the welcome, and then off to the next satellite, where the johns would pay double the going rate for someone who looked as young as she did. Jealousy lashed him, and another dizzying image from *Better Homes and Gardens* flashed before him. Closing his eyes, he shook his head.

"It won't be so bad."

"Did you ever sell yourself for money?"

"No," he said quickly.

"Try it sometime." When she started crying again, the miniskirt and jackboots suddenly looked obscene on her. He felt dizzy and disoriented, not sure of whether he wanted to fuck her or protect her, kill her or kill for her. The one thing stabilizing him was the thought that nobody ever crossed Number One. That reality was a magnet exerting greater and greater force on the needle of his indecision.

"I don't want to try it." The words came easy. "I've already seen what happens to someone who does."

Her face crumbled slowly, like wet sand, and then the rest of her followed. Standing up, he looked down at her huddled body on the bed, a heaving mass of leather and flesh. He started to shake, too, the way he had after the shooting in the pool hall, and he realized he had to leave because the room was so crowded with pain.

Outside, he breathed in fresh air mingled with the faint scent of cow manure, and he wondered when Number One was going to get there. Everything would be all right once he arrived. Number One was the person who found him dealing dime bags on the street and smoking the profits. Number One saw some kind of potential in him, something the Swedish adoptive parents in Wisconsin hadn't seen. They thought they were going to get a wide-eyed and thankful orphan boy, but he had already seen men slaughtered, women gang-raped, and hope lost on a refugee boat that had wandered in the South China Sea for twenty-six days. Merchant ships of all flags ignored them, and a cruise ship blaring disco music sailed by while people came out and looked at them from the railings. Ten years old by the time he arrived in Wisconsin, the damage had been done. He regarded his soul the way a miser did his hoard: never to be shared, never to be spent.

There was nowhere to go but back into the clerk's office. Ramirez sat behind the counter, slowly reading out loud from the sparse print on the scotch bottle's label.

"You look like you need another drink," Ramirez said.

"No, I don't."

"Yes, you do."

The boy dug into his pocket and took out a cigarette pack full of joints. "Thai Stick, very potent—and no paranoia." Ramirez snatched the pack out of his hand so quickly the boy thought he had just performed a magic trick. "Goddammit, I think you took some skin."

"Sorry, my friend!" Sighing happily, Ramirez leaned back in his chair and took out his lighter. After a few joints, the boy was flying so high he thought he might escape gravity itself, and that was when he heard the sound of a car engine. He stood up just in time to see the Nova roar by the office window, and he saw the girl staring right at him, her face dry as concrete. By the time he stumbled out the door, the taillights of the Nova were already dwindling into the empty blackness that surrounded the motel.

"Oh, shit." There was a gun in his hand, but he couldn't remember how it got there or how to put a bullet in the chamber. "Oh, fuck me." A vague memory intruded its way into his mind—he had left his car keys on the nightstand—and he wanted to drop to his knees and start crying. Instead, he ran to the parking lot even though he knew what he was going to find. When he leaned down next to the clerk's pickup, he could hear the steady hiss of air escaping from the tires. The girl had slashed them with his Swiss army knife.

The boy lurched back to the office and found Ramirez lounging in the doorway with a roach between his fingers. The clerk exhaled and coughed. "You two had a bad fight?"

"What the fuck do you think?!" the boy screamed, and it surprised him because he never screamed.

"Calm down. Take a hit. All things will pass."

The boy put the gun in the back of his pants and followed Ramirez into the office. He could feel the gun keeping his back straight even as he wobbled on his feet and stretched out a hand to steady himself. His hand found a switch, and he turned off the lights.

"Hey, what are you doing?"

"Praying."

"What for?"

"A way out."

"Oh, yes." Ramirez sounded wise, but when the boy looked at him, he realized the clerk had already achieved escape velocity. "There's always a way out. God shows the way."

"He isn't showing me a damned thing."

"When God doesn't show you the way out, you look for the back door."

"Don't tell me there's a back door?"

"How can I tell you when you don't ask?"

Ramirez stumbled around the counter and opened the door next to the couch, leading the boy into a room furnished with a twin bed, a steel locker, a table constructed from sawhorses and wooden planks, and a stove. There was another door at the back, and this Ramirez threw open with a grand gesture of his arm, like a magician introducing his lovely assistant. Stepping through the door, the boy entered another world. Instead of the orphaned landscape that surrendered itself at the front door of the motel, there was a tidy garden of sunflowers, each one taller than a man and nodding its head sleepily. The sunflowers stood together in orderly rank and file, helmeted in gold and uniformed in green under the fluorescent light of the moon.

"What do you think, friend?"

"I think you're crazy." The boy had never seen anything so inspired. "I think you're a genius."

"A man's got to do something, surrounded by all this loneliness."

The boy wondered how long it had all taken: the seeding, the cultivation, the watering, and the waiting. The sunflowers stood there like the faithful retainers of a Japanese lord, and the boy knew they would wait forever, but he could not.

"It's time to run, Ramirez."

"My time for running is long gone, my friend."

"You don't get it yet." Leaning close, the boy made sure Ramirez could see his expression under the moonlight. "You stay and they're going to kill you. That's after they torture you to find out where I am."

"Oh." Ramirez blinked, but he evidently wasn't the kind of man who questioned who *they* were. They could be *la migra,* they could be the CIA, they could be the U.S. Marine Corps, they could be aliens in a spaceship. He popped the roach into his mouth and swallowed hard. "You have convinced me that I should start tonight on that long-overdue exercise program. But first, let me get my camera."

They did not run so much as lope through the ranks of sunflowers, weaving back and forth like sailors on a rolling deck. The boy thought of the girl racing through the night in the Love Bug, and he knew that long after this, he would still be able to see her, the way he could look up into the sky and see the light of stars dying and dead. It was amazing to him how inexhaustible light was, and he realized now, as he weaved through the garden of sunflowers, that there was a vast field of stars overhead—more than he ever thought existed and more than he had ever seen in Los Angeles, where only the closest and brightest stars pierced the smog. Over the motel, the air was a transparent window into space, and he felt disoriented, like a traveler looking at the map of an unfamiliar country and feeling overwhelmed by the intricacies of rivers and roads. He knew the stars could be read with the right instruments, just as the Spanish sailed the seas by scanning the night skies, and the Indians looked for signs of fate in their astrology. He wondered if the Spanish thought the Indians were demons when they first saw them, and he wondered if the Indians thought the Spanish were really gods, or if that was only how the Spanish saw themselves in Indian eyes. When he looked at the stars again, he could see only two things spelled out clearly in that vast body of knowledge: fear and hope.

They reached the end of the sunflower bed. Before them, the earth stretched like the flayed skin of a giant—the dry, cracked ground riddled with pores and matted with brown brush. Pausing for breath, they held each other by the shoulders to steady themselves.

"Where now?" The boy was panting.

"Anywhere, my friend." Ramirez spread out his arms as if he wanted to embrace the land. "There's a thousand places to hide. We can live like coyotes or cockroaches."

Neither option appealed to the boy, but he straightened himself up and tried to breathe. He was out of shape and the dope wasn't helping, but he could feel something move inside him. It was his heart kicking back to life and beating on the inside of his chest like a man buried alive. He took a deep breath, and when he heard Ramirez call his name—the stolen one he had entered in the motel ledger—he turned around and was blinded by the flash of the camera. Ramirez giggled in triumph while he returned the Leica to its case, and the boy sighed, rubbing his eyes. As soon as his vision returned, he saw distant car lights heading for the motel. The boy grabbed Ramirez, and together they stumbled and staggered through the moonlit landscape. Rising ahead of them was a small hill, and the boy was certain that from there, he could see what would develop behind him.

About the Contributors

Kevin Bowen served as a soldier in Viet Nam from 1968 to 1969. He is the cotranslator of *Distant Road* by Nguyen Duy, *A Time Far Past* by Luu Le, and *Mountain River: Vietnamese Poetry from the Wars, 1948–1993*. Bowen is also the author of two books of poetry: *Forms of Prayer at the Hotel Edison* and *Playing Basketball with the Viet Cong*. He is the director of the William Joiner Center for the Study of War and Social Consequences at the University of Massachusetts at Boston.

Bradajo (aka Jozuf Hadley) is a third-generation *kamaʻāina* from Kauaʻi. After serving in the air force, he studied art in Oakland, became an art teacher, and then moved to Oʻahu's North Shore in the midsixties. He obtained an MFA in art from the University of Hawaiʻi and, after a life-changing experience in Waimea Canyon, began to write poetry in Hawaiʻi folk talk. His first book, *Chaloookyu Eensai,* was published in 1972. He retired from teaching in 2000.

Don Mee Choi was born in South Korea and came to the United States in 1981. She lives in Seattle and is involved in translating the work of several contemporary Korean women poets. Recent work by her appears in *Arts & Letters: Journal of Contemporary Culture* and *Seneca Review*.

Martha Collins has published four books of poems, the most recent of which is *Some Things Words Can Do* (Sheep Meadow, 1998). *The Women Carry River Water*, a collection of poems by Vietnamese writer Nguyen Quang Thieu, was cotranslated with the author and was published by the University of Massachusetts in 1997. She teaches at Oberlin College.

Linh Dinh was born in Saigon in 1963, came to the United States in 1975, and now divides his time between the States and Viet Nam. He is the author of a collection of stories, *Fake House* (Seven Stories Press, 2000), and three chapbooks of poems, *Drunkard Boxing* (Singing Horse Press, 1998), *A Small Triumph Over Lassitude* (Leroy Press, 2001), and *A Glass of Water* (Skanky Possum Press, 2001). He is also the editor of the anthologies *Night, Again: Contemporary Fiction from Vietnam* (Seven Stories Press, 1996) and *Three Vietnamese Poets* (Tinfish, 2001).

Thuy Dinh is a writer and attorney living in the Washington, D.C., area. Her essays and reviews have appeared in the anthology *Once Upon a Dream: Twenty Years of Vietnamese-American Experience* (Andrews and McMeel, 1995) and the magazines *Amerasia Journal, Rain Taxi Review of Books, Hop Luu,* and *Viet Magnet*.

Do Kh. was born in 1955 in Hai Phong. After studying in Paris in 1974, he decided to return to South Viet Nam, where he enlisted in the army; later, he went back to Paris, where he now lives. His publications include *The Poetry of Do Kh., Unspeakable Chagrins, The Rain-Making Stick, Record of the Trip to the West,* and *Prewar Time.* He cofounded *Hop Luu* journal and *Tap Chi Tho.*

Du Tu Le is the pen name of Le Cu Phach. He was born in 1942 in Ha Nam Province, moved to the South between 1954 and 1955, and now lives in the United States. In 1973, he received the first prize in literature given by the Republic of South Viet Nam. One of the most prolific poets living in exile, he has written over thirty works of poetry and prose. Some of his recent collections of poetry are *Looking at Each Other, We See Mountains and Rivers, Love Poems, What Cries/On the Other Side of the Weather,* and *Reflection in the Looking Glass.* Many of his poems have been set to music.

George Evans served as a medic in Viet Nam. His poetry has been widely acclaimed and anthologized; his most recent collection is *The New World* (Curbstone Press, 2002). He is also a translator and novelist. His story in this issue is excerpted from his novel in progress, *A Year without Sleep.* He lives in San Francisco.

H. E. Francis has published short fiction and translations in numerous journals as well as in *The O. Henry Awards, The Pushcart Prize: Best of the Small Presses,* and *Best American Short Stories.* His most recently published novel is *The Invisible Country.* He divides his time between Huntsville, Alabama, and Madrid.

Frank Gerke was born in 1965 in Germany and studied Chinese and Vietnamese in Berlin and Bonn. He worked as a research fellow at the Federal Institute for Eastern and International Studies in Cologne and then studied for many years in Viet Nam, publishing several literary works in Vietnamese. A lecturer in the department of South East Asian studies at the University of Bonn, he focuses on modern Vietnamese and Chinese literature.

Guo Lusheng is the given name of the poet Shi Zhi. Born in 1948, he is revered as a forerunner of post-Mao avant-garde poetry and has been compared to Dante and Ezra Pound. A collection of his poetry was published in Beijing in 1993.

Hoang Lien was a civilian governor in South Viet Nam. Captured by North Vietnamese troops during the Tet Offensive of 1968, he was imprisoned until 1980. He came to the United States in 1984 and subsequently published his prison poems in a collection entitled *Sitting Still.* His prison memoir, *Light and Darkness,* was published in 1990; he also wrote two collections of short stories, *Between Two Horizons* and *Crazed.* In November 2000, he died in San Francisco of cancer.

Huu Thinh was born in the hamlet of Phu Vinh in 1942. A combat veteran of the Vietnamese-American War, he is one of the most important poets of his generation and the recipient of many literary prizes in Viet Nam. The longtime editor-in-chief of the magazine *Van Nghe,* he lives in Ha Noi and is deputy general secretary of the Viet Nam Writers' Association. The poems in this issue are from *The Time Tree* (Curbstone Press, 2002), a bilingual edition of his poetry.

Ko Ŭn is one of South Korea's most prominent poets. He became a Buddhist monk in 1952, during the Korean War, but after ten years, he left the monastic life and became a schoolteacher. During the 1970s and 1980s, he was politically active in the workers' and pro-democratic movements. He wrote prolifically during that time, producing the multivolume *Paektusan* (White Mountain), an epic historical poem that depicts Korea's independence movement during the Japanese occupation.

Andrew Lam is an associate editor for the Pacific News Service and a regular commentator on National Public Radio's series *All Things Considered.* Currently a Knight fellow at Stanford University, he is working on his first short-story collection.

Lam Thi My Da was born in 1949 in Quang Binh Province and now lives in Hue. During the war, she served in Quang Tri and Thua Thien with the youth brigades and the women's engineering units. She is an executive board member of the Viet Nam Writers' Association and the Vietnamese Women's Association. Her most recent book of poems, *De tan mot giac mo* (Dedicated to a dream), was published in 1998 and won highest honors from the National United Board of Vietnamese Literature and the Arts.

Christian Langworthy received a commission as a lieutenant in the United States Army in 1990. His work will appear in the forthcoming anthologies: *In the Mix, Bold Words,* and *Vietnamese American Literature 1975–2000.* His poems and fiction appear in such literary journals and forums as PBS American Experience, Salon.com, *Asian-Pacific American Journal, Muae,* and *Viet Nam Forum.*

Le Bi is the pen name of Hoang Chinh Nghia. He was born in 1949 in North Viet Nam and went south in 1954. An officer in the Army of the Republic of South Viet Nam, he resettled in the United States in 1975. A writer of free verse, he has published two collections of poetry, *Cited Poetry* and *A Person's Address.* He now resides in Southern California.

Mai Thao is the pen name of Nguyen Dang Quy. He was born in 1927 in Nam Dinh. When the Ho Chi Minh government took over the North in 1954, he joined the exodus south. He became a key figure in the pre-1975 literature of South Viet Nam and was one of the main contributors to *Sang Tao* (Creativity) and *Nghe Thuat* (Arts) journals. In 1978, he resettled in the United States and founded *Van* (Literature), the first major literary journal produced by Vietnamese overseas. A prolific author with ten collections of short stories, thirty-three novels, and two personal narratives, he died in 1998. He is best remembered for his volume of verse, *We See in Our Form the Shape of Temples and Shrines.*

John McKernan has recently published poems in *West Branch, Georgia Review,* and *Paris Review.*

Joseph Millar lives in western Oregon, where he teaches at Mount Hood Community College. His poems have appeared in recent issues of *Shenandoah, Ploughshares,* and *Mānoa.* His first collection, *Overtime,* appeared last year from Eastern Washington University Press.

Mộng-Lan is a visual artist and writer whose first book of poems, *Song of the Cicadas,* won the 2000 Juniper Prize and was published by the University of Massachusetts Press. Her poem in this issue is from a recently completed book, *in the instant.*

Leonard Nathan recently published *The Potato Eaters* (Orchises Press, 1999), which was awarded a silver medal for poetry by the Commonwealth Club of California, and *Diary of a Left-Handed Birdwatcher* (Harcourt Brace, 1998). He has published in the magazines *Atlantic, The New Yorker,* and *Mānoa,* among others.

 Mike Ngo is a prisoner in San Quentin and a political activist, writer, and intellectual.

 Nguyen Ba Chung is a poet, translator, and essayist. He was born in 1949 in Kim Thanh District, Hai Duong Province, and moved to Saigon with his family in 1955. In 1971, after attending the Faculty of Letters in Saigon, he came to the United States to pursue a graduate degree in American literature at Brandeis University. He has been a research associate at the William Joiner Center for the Study of War and Social Consequences at the University of Massachusetts at Boston since 1996 and is the author of four collections of poetry in Vietnamese and the cotranslator of numerous volumes into English.

 Nguyen Duy was born in 1948 in Thanh Hoa Province. Among his many awards are the *Van Nghe* poetry prize given in 1973 and the poetry prize given by the Viet Nam Writers' Association in 1985. One of the most traveled writers both inside and outside Viet Nam, he has visited the United States three times. He has published ten collections of poetry, three memoirs, and a novel; his collection *Distant Road* was published by Curbstone Press in 1999.

 Nguyen Minh Chau was born in 1930 in Nghe An. Along with the critic Hoang Ngoc Hien, he was the earliest champion of *doi moi* (renovation) literature, publishing in 1978 an essay called "Writing about War," which had a tremendous influence on writers. His books include *The River Mouth, In the Footsteps of a Soldier,* and *Land of Passion.* A colonel in the North Vietnamese army, he died in 1989 in Ha Noi of liver cancer contracted through wartime exposure to chemical defoliants.

 Phung Nguyen is the author of two collections of short stories, *The Tower of Memories* (1998) and *Oakland Night and Other Stories* (2001). His short stories have been published in numerous Vietnamese literary magazines, including *Van Hoc, Van,* and *Hop Luu* in the United States and *Viet Magazine* in Australia. A former soldier in the South Vietnamese army, he came to the United States in 1984 and now lives and works in Bakersfield, California.

 Nguyen Qui Duc is the author of *Where the Ashes Are: The Odyssey of a Vietnamese Family* (Addison-Wesley, 1994) and the coeditor, with John Balaban, of *Vietnam: A Traveler's Literary Companion* (Whereabouts Press, 1995). His short stories and essays have been published in numerous anthologies and journals, and he is the translator of the novel *Behind the Red Mist* (Curbstone Press, 1998) by Ha Noi writer Ho Anh Thai. His translation of Huu Thinh's book of poetry, *The Time*

Tree, was published in spring 2002. He currently hosts *Pacific Time,* a National Public Radio program focusing on Asia and its connections to America.

Nguyen Thi Kieu Thu was born in Saigon in 1958. After graduating from the University of Ho Chi Minh City, she became a teacher of English there. In 1995, she attended the University of Massachusetts at Boston to obtain her master's degree. She is now a lecturer on British and American literature in the department of English, linguistics, and literature at the University of Social Sciences and Humanities in Ho Chi Minh City.

Viet Thanh Nguyen was born in Viet Nam and came to the United States in 1975. Educated at the University of California at Berkeley, he is an assistant professor of English and Asian American studies at the University of Southern California. He is the author of *Race and Resistance: Literature and Politics in Asian America* (Oxford University Press).

Juan Carlos Onetti twice won the National Prize from Uruguay and the Cervantes award from Spain, the most coveted literary award after the Nobel Prize. His work has been translated into numerous languages. He is especially known for creating the fictional world of Santa Maria (his Yoknapatawpha County) and for his literary style.

Phan Nhien Hao was born in 1970 in Kontum. He immigrated to the United States in 1991 and now lives in San Jose, California. He graduated in Vietnamese literature from the Teachers College of Saigon and in American literature from the University of California at Los Angeles. He has been publishing poems, stories, and translations in literary journals since 1989 and is the author of *Paradise of Paper Bells,* a poetry collection. His poems have been translated into English and published in the journals *Literary Review* and *Filling Station* and in the anthology *Vietnam Inside Out: A Dialogue* (St. Martin's Press, 2001).

Phon-anh was director of an independent survey research institute in Saigon and taught social science methodology at the University of Dalat. He was awarded the 1987 Grand Pris Littéraire International for his poem *Pourquoi Me Réveiller,* which is about a thirteen-year-old Vietnamese girl who survived an attack at sea by bandits in the Gulf of Thailand. He is now retired and lives in Houston, Texas.

Virgil Suárez was born in Havana in 1962 and is the author of *Palm Crows,* a collection of poems exploring memories of Cuba (University of Arizona Press, 2001). His other publications include *Welcome to the Oasis, Spared Angola: Memories from a Cuban-American Childhood, Banyan,* and *Guide to the Blue Tongue.*

Barbara Tran is the coeditor of *Watermark: Vietnamese American Poetry & Prose* and the recipient of a Pushcart Prize. Her poetry manuscript, *In the Mynah Bird's Own Words,* was the winner of the Tupelo Press chapbook competition, judged by Robert Wrigley. It was published in early 2002.

Tran Tien Dung was born in Go Cong in 1957 and now lives in Ho Chi Minh City. He is the author of two volumes of poetry, *Moving Mass* (1997) and *Appear* (2000). His appearance in this issue is his first in English.

Truong Tran was born in 1969 in Saigon. He and his family emigrated to the United States and settled in the San Francisco Bay Area. He is the recipient of poetry fellowships from the Arts Council of Santa Clara, the California Arts Council, and the Creative Work Fund Grant. His first collection of poems, *The Book of Perceptions,* was a finalist for the Kiriyama Book Prize, and his second collection, *Placing the Accents,* was a finalist for the Western States Book Prize. His poems in this issue are reprinted from *dust and conscience* (Apogee Press, 2002). He lives in San Francisco, where he teaches writing.

 Trinh Cong Son was born in Viet Nam's Central Highlands in 1939. Trained as a teacher, he started writing songs in the late 1950s, favoring lyrics about human emotions and, later, the tragedy of war. His popularity soared during the 1960s and 1970s, although his songs were suppressed by the governments of both North and South Viet Nam. After the war, the new government sentenced him to four years of reeducation in the labor camps. His songs returned to wide distribution and popularity in the 1980s and 1990s. He died in April 2001 at the age of sixty-two. During his lifetime, he composed about seven hundred songs.

Michelle Yeh is a professor in the department of East Asian languages and cultures at the University of California at Davis. Her most recent publications are *Essays on Modern Chinese Poetry* (1998); *No Trace of the Gardener: Poems of Yang Mu* (1998), cotranslated with Lawrence R. Smith; *From the Margin: An Alternative Tradition of Modern Chinese Poetry* (2000); and *Frontier Taiwan: An Anthology of Modern Chinese Poetry* (2001), coedited with N. G. D. Malmqvist. Her translation of "My Last Beijing" first appeared in *Modern China* in October 1992.

Zhang Lijia is a freelance journalist whose articles have appeared in such places as the *South China Morning Post, Japan Times, Washington Times,* and *Newsweek.* She is the coauthor of *China Remembers,* an oral history of the People's Republic of China (Oxford University Press, 1999).